John Hampden Burnham

Canadians in the Imperial Naval And Military Service Abroad

John Hampden Burnham
Canadians in the Imperial Naval And Military Service Abroad
ISBN/EAN: 9783744725408

Printed in Europe, USA, Canada, Australia, Japan

Cover: Foto ©ninafisch / pixelio.de

More available books at **www.hansebooks.com**

CANADIANS

IN THE

IMPERIAL
NAVAL AND MILITARY SERVICE
ABROAD.

BY
J. HAMPDEN BURNHAM, M.A.,
of Osgoode Hall, Barrister-at-Law.

"Canadians have shown, on more than one memorable occasion, that in military spirit they are not wanting."—THE POLITICAL DESTINY OF CANADA, by *Goldwin Smith*, D.C.L

Toronto:
WILLIAMSON & CO., 5 KING STREET WEST.
LONDON: W. H. ALLEN & Co., 13 WATERLOO PLACE, S.W.
1891.

Dedicated

BY

GRACIOUS PERMISSION

TO

HIS EXCELLENCY

The Governor General of Canada,

LORD STANLEY OF PRESTON,

BY

THE AUTHOR.

PREFACE.

CANADIANS, if they know their country, do not know their countrymen so intimately as they might. The histories of Canada are numerous and elaborate, but the same cannot be said with regard to the histories of Canadians. The remark refers more particularly to those of our countrymen who have entered the naval and military services of the Empire, and have gone abroad.

In visiting the chief libraries it was found that information concerning the subject of this little book is surprisingly scant.

For this reason the writer resolved to undertake the pleasant duty of gathering from authentic sources such details as exist. Though in the course of the time occupied, nearly three years, he has travelled over twelve thousand miles in search of trustworthy testimony, that testimony is unfortunately incomplete. He has proceeded on the principle of admitting only that which he had ascertained to be true, and rejecting altogether mere tradition or hearsay. Literary excellence has not been the first consideration. The necessity of some work of this sort became the more manifest as time went on. Naval and military men and others received very favourably a serious attempt at giving some historical account of their services. The writer felt that travelling to and fro simply in Canada would not accomplish the object in view. He therefore went to England and spent a considerable time in the British Museum, in conning over the naval, military, and public records of Great Britain, and in journeying about that country for the purpose of gathering material.

The collection of materials in England was rendered most agreeable both by the cordiality of Englishmen and their kind interest in the matter, and by the active sympathy displayed by many of the Canadians resident in England. It is the writer's wish to acknowledge most gratefully the obligations he is under to those Englishmen, Scotchmen, and Irishmen with whom he had the pleasure of coming in contact, as well as to the Canadians, whose assistance he has received. The number of names is much larger than by this book appears, and until those who possess information, and of whom the writer has not heard, send in not only new names but more details, nothing complete and worthy of the subject can be put together.

Quotations have been used extensively because it is only too easy to be vain-glorious, and because it has been the writer's object to approach the subject from an Imperial point of view.

If readers regard with favour this earnest endeavour to present authentically what has, in great part, been neglected of late, it is hoped that they will forward to the writer such information as they possess. Even clues which may be followed up are of some value.

It is a sort of treason to the spirit of a people that the memories of the brave should remain uncherished. Many Canadians have had honourable careers abroad, in the service of peace, but those are not here treated of—the Archibalds who became judges of the High Court in England, Sir William Winniett, Sir Samuel Cunard, "the father of Atlantic steam-navigation," &c.

Much assistance has been given by some of the most prominent men of the Dominion, who have taken up the subject with a heartiness that has been most gratifying. To many of these the writer's plans were submitted, and the publication of concise sketches as a step towards an elaboration at some future time, has been approved of by those before whom it has been laid. The writer will be content if his efforts as compiler and scribe are thought to form a substantial beginning, and for the interest taken in the work and assistance given, he wishes to thank most sincerely the following ladies and gentlemen :— Lady Darling, Lady Willshire, Mrs. Robinson-Owen; Miss. Harriet E. Boulton, of Toronto; the Right Honourable Sir John A. Macdonald, P.C.,G.C.B.,G.C. M.G., Premier of Canada; Sir Charles Tupper, Bart., G.C.B.,G.C.M.G., High Commissioner for Canada in London; Goldwin Smith, Esqr., D.C.L., Sir Andrew Stuart, the Hon. Henri G. Joly de Lotbinière, Sir Adams Archibald, the Hon. Mr. Justice Baby, Martin Griffin, Esqr., Librarian of House of Commons of Canada; F. B. Crofton, Esqr., Librarian of Legislature at Halifax; Silas Farmer, Esqr., Historiographer, of Michigan, U. S., the Hon. Charles H. Tupper, Minister of Marine and Fisheries; Christopher Robinson, Esqr., Q.C., Major-General Cameron, C.M.G., Commandant of the Royal Military College of Kingston, Canada; Major Todd, Major Mayne, R.E., Captain Forbes, R.N., T. Akin, Esqr., Archivist, of Nova Scotia; M. Sulte, Douglas Brymner, Esqr., Dominion Archivist; Colonel Duchesnay, D.A.G., Herbert Forlong, Esqr., Major Crawford Lindsay, Colonel Montizambert and Major Wilson, of the Citadel at Quebec; J. Le Moine, Esqr., F.R.S.C., Major Vidal, V.C. Surgeon-General Reade, James P. Cleghorn, Esqr., of Montreal; the Mayor of Halifax, Lt.-Col. Bremner, E. J. Toker, Esqr., of the

Empire; the officers of the Admiralty Office, of the War Office, of the Public Records Office, of the Paymaster-General's Office, of the Rolls Office, of the Historical Society of Quebec, and to very many others, and especially to Mr. J. W. O'Brien, of the Newspaper Department of the British Museum, late of the 4th Dragoon Guards, whose great information on all naval and military matters, and accurate acquaintance with the proper sources of that information, were invaluable.

The following is from a letter of Sir Adams Archibald:

HALIFAX, October 15, 1890.

MY DEAR SIR, ... I congratulate you on the selection of the subject for your book, and am sure it will fill a space that ought to be filled. It will require a good deal of labour and trouble, but it ought to be, and I doubt not will be, welcomed by every true Canadian.

Believe me, my dear sir,
with best wishes,
yours very faithfully,
(Sgd.) A. G. ARCHIBALD.

J. Hampden Burnham, Esqr.,
Peterborough, Ont.

These sketches are confined to commissioned officers.

J. H. B.

PETERBOROUGH,
December 1st, 1890.

CANADIANS

IN THE

IMPERIAL SERVICE ABROAD.

H.M. 100TH REGIMENT.

IN past times the regard of Canadians for British traditions and for the motherland has shown itself in many ways. The love of the home of their ancestors has been nourished by them with all steadfastness, as is natural in an independent and a loyal people.*
This sentiment has flourished, it may well be said, because the trend of British institutions has been toward a more extensive liberty and to a more enduring

---

* "Another thing that struck him was the independence of Canadians. Something of this was, no doubt, due to our educational system; something was due to the sociability engendered by our bracing climate, and a great deal was due to our local government, which seemed to him absolutely perfect." Mr. John T. Wood, one of the Farmers' delegates from Britain, at Calgary, Oct. 10, 1890, in reply, on behalf of the delegation, as reported in the *Empire*.

civilization. The proof of this is in the attachment of the descendants of the French in Canada to Britain, and in the confederation of the Dominion itself.

There underlies this, too, an honesty of purpose—a just intention—in the true heart of the race that has preserved this allegiance—an allegiance that is a tribute to her principles of which Britain, herself, may well be proud. Instances may occur again where the folly of rulers may cause an unpremeditated separation, but this will not be in accordance with the genius of Imperial development. No other empire has ever had colonies so great in magnitude and in number, nor has any bound them to herself by bonds so fragile yet so strong.

Other nations have been deprived of theirs by the continuous storms of tumult and rebellion, but Britain has preserved her dependencies for, in general, she has given them the most ample liberty and protection.

It is in no sense the worst part of a people that braves the perils of sea and land in quest of settlement, and England's colonists have shown that they have not lost the ancient spirit—that their inheritance is not wasted in their hands, and that their rough-hewn destiny is shaping to a successful future.

In times of need, an offer of men has, more than once, been made by Canada, and as many times accepted, but the first offer of national importance was at the outbreak of the last great war with Russia. Nor has she been ungenerous in the matter of money.

For very many years the press of England has referred to Canada in kindly acknowledgment of assistance offered and given.

For a century or more, the chief organs of public opinion* have spoken frequently upon the importance of "the premier colony" to the Empire, and, if the time come to begin the career of an independent nation, Canada may justly feel that she has not been recreant to a sacred duty.

When the immediate cause of the rise of the 100th regiment—the Crimean War—no longer existed, and the Indian Mutiny had been suppressed, the regiment was given garrison duty. When the new territorial system was adopted, the 100th lost its distinctively Canadian name.

At the present time, the first battalion of the corps is the *old* 100th regiment.

---

* See the *Times* for the last one hundred years. Also the *Military and Naval Gazette*, etc., etc.

THE PRINCE OF WALES'S LEINSTER REGIMENT (ROYAL CANADIAN).

1st Battalion : (Prince of Wales's Royal Canadian Regt.) late 100th Regt.

2nd Battalion : (Bombay Infantry) late 109th Regt.

TERRITORIAL BADGES :—On the buttons—a circle inscribed " Prince of Wales's Leinster Regiment."

Within the Circle :—The Prince of Wales's Plume.

On the Collars :—The Prince of Wales's Plume in silver, the coronet gilt-metal.

On the Helmet-Plates :—In silver, on a ground of black velvet, forming the centre of the regulation-pattern, gilt-star and wreath, the Prince of Wales's Plume over two Maple Leaves, emblematic of the Provinces of Upper Canada and Lower Canada, now Ontario and Quebec.

On a scroll beneath the Maple Leaves :—" Central India." On the universal scroll :—" Prince of Wales's Leinster Regiment."

Waist-Plates :—Special pattern with Maple Leaf ends : in silver on a burnished gilt centre—a Maple and Laurel wreath.

Within the Wreath :—A circle inscribed, " The Leinster Regiment."

Above the Circle :—The Crown : within it, the Prince of Wales's Plumes ; below it, on a wreath, a deadgilt scroll inscribed, " Central India."

On the round forage-caps:—The Prince of Wales's Plume in silver with scroll and motto in gilt-metal. Below the Plume—a scroll in gilt-metal inscribed, "The Leinster."

Lace :—Gold—Shamrock pattern.

BATTALION " QUEEN'S" COLOURS :—The Union throughout, with the regimental title in letters of gold on a crimson centre, according to regulation, and the Crown over.

BATTALION " REGIMENTAL " COLOURS :—Blue with the battalion number in the first corner; in each of the others a Maple Leaf.

The Prince of Wales's Plume is borne on a crimson centre surrounded by the Crown. The titles and battle-honours according to regulation.

The number "100th," formerly borne by the first battalion of the present regiment, has belonged, in all, to six different regiments in the Imperial service. Of these, two are intimately connected with Canadian history. The last of the six is the one now known as the "Leinster Regiment," which " owed its origin to Canadian loyalty, at the period of the Indian Mutiny." *

When the Crimean War began, and Great Britain was very much in need of men, several Canadian gentlemen offered the Home Government a regiment

---

* *English Magazine.*

from Canada, but it was found impossible to accept then, as the attention of the authorities was engrossed in placing in the field the regiments that were ready for action, as well as in watching the movements of Russia. The offer was, however, borne in mind and, at the outbreak of the Indian Mutiny, was accepted.

The regiment was at once placed upon the regular strength of the army and was styled the "100th, or Prince of Wales's Royal Canadian Regiment," to be one thousand strong. Recruiting began at once. Great care was taken that no citizens of the United States should enlist, as the Home Government did not wish to become embroiled with that nation, in this respect, as had occurred once before.

Under the regulations then recently introduced the commissions were not purchasable, though their value was to be the same as in other regiments. The lieutenant-colonel, one major, six captains, and six lieutenants were appointed from the Canadian Active Militia —preference being given to those who had previously offered their services, and who brought forward recruits. Four ensigns were appointed from those who had passed, with honors, the examinations of the Royal Canadian Military College.

Baron de Rottenburg, the adjutant-general of the Canadian Militia, was made lieutenant-colonel of the regiment; ꝶ.ℭ. Lieut. Alexander Roberts Dunn, a native of Toronto and a former officer of the 11th Hussars, was appointed to the majority.

The recruits were enrolled at the five chief cities of the two provinces of Ontario and Quebec. The first step towards formation was taken in April, 1858, and by the end of the following month the regiment was in quarters in the citadel at Quebec, awaiting embarkation for England.

It was in every sense a fine corps. The men were of splendid physique, inured to fatigue, well-equipped, and ready for the fray. It arrived in England in three detachments and was stationed at Shorncliffe. Major-general Viscount Melville, K.C.B., a very distinguished officer, was made colonel of the " Royal Canadians." In an editorial of May 27th, 1858, upon the coming of the regiment, the *Times* said : " The event will be not a little remarkable, for it will constitute, we believe, the very first example of its kind in the history of the British Army. . . . . . At length the colonial corps of various descriptions have become recognized as members of our ordinary military establishments. . . . . Even a Canadian regiment is no new formation, for we have already a Royal Canadian rifle regiment, one thousand strong, borne on the general rolls of Her Majesty's Land Forces. .

Notwithstanding the aggregate increase in the numbers of the Army, this new battalion represents the only regimental addition to the strength of the Line. . . But the precedent is instructive as well as remarkable, in the pledge it offers of the loyalty and good affection of the Canadians.

"Our military establishments have often been sorely taxed for the wants of the colonies, but this is the first time that the colonies have added to the regular resources of the army. The men of the new regiment are spoken of as an efficient and soldierlike body, and there cannot, of course, be the slightest reason why they should not be a match for any other corps in the service. . . . . An established and recognized connection with a country or province—such as the 100th Regiment will preserve with Canada—would tend to give the youth of the district both an interest in the corps and an inducement to enter it."

On the 8th of September, His Royal Highness the Duke of Cambridge reviewed the troops in which the Canadian regiment was. On this occasion he was accompanied by Her Royal Highness the Duchess of Cambridge, and the Princess Mary. The appearance of the men was excellent. When his Royal Highness came upon the ground he proceeded immediately to the right of the 100th Regiment, which stood somewhat apart for the purpose of being inspected. " On riding down the line, the Duke expressed himself as highly pleased with the men, and praised their soldierlike appearance in such language as, ' what splendid men!' 'What a fine regiment!'"* His Royal Highness having commanded them to form " column " and " square," and having tested them in further movements, addressed them as follows :—

" Colonel de Rottenburg, I daresay you have been surprised that I have not been down to see you before this, but I was desirous that you should have an opportunity of equipping your men—that you should have a short time for drill, and I see that I was not mistaken. You have evidently taken advantage of the time given you, for the appearance of your regiment not only proves your ability as a commander but fully exemplifies the intelligence of the men. I am very much pleased with the manner in which they have formed 'column' and 'square.' It has been done with the steadiness of old soldiers.

"Soldiers of the 100th, or Royal Canadian Regiment, I am glad at having this opportunity of addressing you. I can assure you it gives me great pleasure to meet such a fine body of men, so well equipped and

---

*London Gazette, 1858.

in such a good state of discipline. I speak as a military man and call upon my Right Honorable friend the Secretary of State for War, who will, I am sure, corroborate my assertion, more especially when it is considered that the regiment was raised in so short a time—raised in the hour of trial, when danger menaced England. Then Canadian gentlemen nobly and manfully volunteered to serve. Both are equally deserving of my thanks. Raising a regiment at such a time and under such circumstances is, militarily speaking, very gratifying, and I think my Right Honorable friend will say, speaking politically, it merits special consideration. . . . . I am sure the 100th, wherever they may be, will do honor to themselves and honor to Canada, and, in honoring Canada, do honor to England. . . . . ."

After the address, under the Duke's command, the regiment was again put through a series of movements, which drew forth his warm approval of its quickness and proficiency.

On the 6th of November, the 100th received orders to make ready for active service in India, but, to its disappointment, the service was not required. It was ordered instead to proceed to Gibraltar.

Before leaving Shorncliffe, the Prince of Wales presented the regiment with its "colours," which were inscribed with the word "Niagara," borne by the old 100th regiment, and also by some of the regiments of the militia of Canada, in memory of the share taken by them in that desperate fight.

Having done duty at Gibraltar, and afterwards at Malta, the regiment was ordered back to England. Upon the lapse of the usual period at home after foreign station, the regiment was sent to Bengal in 1877, subsequently being placed at Fort William, where it remained.

On the 21st of February, 1887, Lady Dufferin presented the first battalion of what is now known as "The Leinster or Prince of Wales's Royal Canadian Regiment," with new "colours" at Calcutta.

The occasion was celebrated by a grand ball given at the Town Hall. Amongst those who were present were Their Excellencies, the Viceroy and Lady Dufferin, His Honour the Lieutenant-Governor and Lady Rivers Thompson, His Excellency, the Commander-in-chief and the "élite of Calcutta." The old colours, that had been with them twenty-nine years, were placed in a prominent position at the end of the Hall, under the charge of private Dagas, one of the old French-Canadian soldiers who had joined the regiment at the time of its organization in 1858.

These colours are now at Ottawa as a memorial of the band of English and French-Canadians who sprang to the Empire's aid in time of peril and foreboding. In handing the new ones over to the custody of the regiment, the Countess of Dufferin said: "Colonel MacKinnon, officers, non-commissioned officers and men of the Royal Canadians:—The regiment to which you have the honor to belong, rose into existence in the time of England's greatest need —owed itsbirth to the loyal devotion of our Canadian fellow-subjects, and its embodiment was one of the earliest indications given by our colonists of that determination they have so universally expressed to recognize and maintain the unity and common interest of the British Empire. I now entrust these colours to your guardianship, fully believing that you will rally round them nobly and gallantly in whatever quarter of the world they may be displayed, in defence of England's honor and the Queen's dominions."

List of officers of the 100th *Regiment, in* 1858.

Colonel.—Henry, Viscount Melville, K.C.B.
Lt.-Col.—George, Baron de Rottenburg, C.B.
Majors.—Jas. Henry Craig Robertson.
     V.C. Alexander Roberts Dunn.
Captains—
     Tho. Maths. LuzWeg. uelin.
     Robert Bethune Ingram.

Captains—
> Percy G. Botfield Lake.
> Henry Cooke.
> Jas. Clery.
> Henry Geo. Browne.

Lieutenants—
> Geo. Bell Coulson.
> John Lee.
> Jas. Lamb.
> Fred William Benwell.
> Henry Lionel Nicholls.
> Jos. Dooley.
> Rich. Lane Bayliff.
> Charles Boulton.

Paymaster—Jas. Hutchison.
Quartermaster—Geo. Grant.

GENERAL SIR WILLIAM FENWICK WILLIAMS, BART., G.C.B.

ROYAL ARTILLERY.

IN the issue of April 3rd, 1858, *The Illustrated London News* represents, by two wood-cuts, the birth-places of General Williams and General Inglis, with the following remarks: "Nova Scotia is justly proud of having contributed, from a population of three hundred thousand, several illustrious names to the roll of national heroes. Chief among the sons whom she delights to honor, may be mentioned Major-General Sir John Inglis, C.B., and his gallant uncle, General Cochrane; Sir W. F. Williams, of Kars; Major Wellsford, who led the assault and was the first to fall in the Redan at the capture of Sebastopol, and Capt. Parker, who fell on the same occasion. We have engraved from sketches, kindly forwarded to us by a resident of Halifax, the cottages in which two of this gallant band were born. The first engraving represents the house in which Sir W. F. Williams, of Kars, was born. It is a quaint wooden structure in the old village of Annapolis

Major-Gen. Sir W. F. Williams, of Kars, Bart.

Royal. Near at hand, in what was once the ditch of the old fort, but now the church-yard, lie the successful general's father and grandfather, the wife of the latter, the daughter of that old colonial soldier, Jeffry, Lord Amherst.

"The second engraving represents the house where Sir J. Inglis was born. It is in Halifax, and was the residence of his father and grandfather, both Bishops of Nova Scotia.

"This house is also of wood, an ordinary cottage with wings, containing library and drawing-room. An address has recently been passed by the two Houses of the Provincial Parliament of Nova Scotia to Major-General Sir John Inglis."

GENERAL WILLIAMS.

WILLIAM FENWICK WILLIAMS was born on the fourth day of December, in the year 1800, at Annapolis in Nova Scotia.

He was the son of the late Thomas Williams, Esquire, of Halifax in the same province, and, by the death of an elder brother in the Battle of New Orleans, he was left the sole-surviving one.

After a preliminary course at Woolwich, where he passed his examinations with credit, he entered the Royal Artillery at the age of twenty-five as second lieutenant. On the 16th of November, 1827, he became first-lieutenant, and second-captain on the 13th of August, 1840.

His career at Woolwich made a favorable impression and he was chosen as special engineer at Ceylon, where he remained for nine years. This appointment was made shortly after his leaving Woolwich.

So faithfully had he done his duty at this post, that he was selected to act in concert with the British ambassador at Constantinople, in settling the disputes as to boundaries between Persia and Turkey.

In this position he was required to act with great judgment and diplomatic tact. His success marked him as a most available man in these Asiatic complications. During the period occupied in these negotiations, Captain Williams dwelt for the most part in a tent, and as a consequence his health suffered from exposure. In addition to this, the robber-bands that infested the district attacked him frequently, and caused him ceaseless anxiety.

Then he was appointed " Superintendent of Turkish Military Arsenals," with a position in the Embassy. This he held for three years. In this large field he was of especial usefulness not only to Turkey and England, but also to Western Europe. Lord Granville thanked him publicly, and on the 22nd of May, 1846, he was gazetted a Major of the Army. At this juncture, 1847, Russia was endeavoring to become embroiled with Persia and Turkey for her own benefit in Asia. Major Williams was dispatched with large powers, to compromise, and, if possible, prevent this. For three years the negotiations were carried on, but his patience was equal to his firmness and he succeeded.

In 1848, he was raised to the rank of lieutenant-colonel and remained as Her Majesty's Commissioner, to carry through what was known as "The Stipulation of Erzeroum," which he had a prominent part in framing. In 1852 he was made a "Companion of the Bath," and in the following year, lieutenant-colonel of the Royal Artillery.

England has always, since the acquisition of her Indian possessions, been compelled to watch untiringly the movements of Russia. With much cunning and zeal the Czar had corrupted the peoples in Central Asia, so that their rulers were merely his hirelings, yet the people themselves were not wholly blind to his sinister designs. To counteract the influence of Russia, it was deemed expedient to protect and assist the tribes of Asia Minor.

At the outbreak of the Crimean war, there were two large forts in Armenia—Erzeroum and Kars.

In the year 1854, Turkey had gone through the form

of putting these places in proper condition, but it was a failure.

Recognizing the vast importance of these places and the weakness of the Sultan, England resolved to undertake the fortifications herself, with what success, shall be seen. Lord Clarendon, the Minister of Foreign Affairs, chose Colonel Williams as best fitted for the task. The latter was instructed to act as Her Majesty's Commissioner at Headquarters with the Turkish forces, and the rank of " Brigadier-General " was conferred upon him. Without delay, he proceeded to Erzeroum and thence to Kars, " a city whose name he was destined to render famous, through all time, in the annals of English military exploits."*

Kars is in the Arpa chain of mountains in Asiatic Turkey, about one hundred and sixty miles to the north-east of Erzeroum. It is a picturesque and striking city, situate at the foot of high cliffs. In the middle of it stands a great mediæval castle, upon a lofty hill. The houses of the city were built chiefly of mud, and stretched away to a considerable distance. A river runs through it about mid-way, and a large ravine cuts through the high hills in the rear. The name of the river is Kars-Chai, or Mountain-River. The castle is near the Kars-Chai, and had been, in feudal times, a place of great strength. A fine stone bridge spanned

* English Newspaper.

the river, close to the castle. Throughout the place indications of Persian architecture, as it once was, were scattered in profusion, forming a singular contrast to the mud huts.

This is the city that General Williams undertook to defend. He saw that much had to be done to render it capable of defence. Undiscouraged by the prospect, an elaborate system of fortifications was drawn up. It was given to Lieutenant Teesdale to carry out.

Though the means were quite insufficient and the outlook gloomy, the officers boldly faced the task and did not rest till Kars assumed the aspect of a modern fortress.

In course of time Colonel Lake, R.E., succeeded Lieut. Teesdale, and was named by the Russians the English "Todtleben."

Whilst these defences were progressing at Kars, General Williams went to Erzeroum. This city is surrounded by lofty mountains, and is, itself, upon a hill. The pashas in and about, like the Armenians in general, had become friendly to the Russians, and were in a continual ferment of jealous strife. This strife it was necessary to pacify before the fortifications could be proceeded with.

At this moment, the jealousy of Lord Stratford de Redcliffe, the British Ambassador at Constantinople, for the first time blazed forth. He would send General Williams neither supplies nor munitions of war, and, amidst a cloud of falsehoods and baseless excuses, left the General to what, he hoped, was total failure.

The affairs of great nations are not easily managed, but that this man should have been left as ambassador at Constantinople, during this period, is of a piece with the fitting-out of the British expedition to the Crimea. This cruel desertion became noised abroad, and to a large extent rendered General Williams's efforts of small avail. In this plight, on the first day of June, 1855, he received a despatch from Colonel Lake that the Russians were advancing in large numbers. He hastened to Kars with all speed.

The garrison was composed of fifteen thousand men, of whom a small number were British troops, the others being Turks and Armenian allies. The artillery, which in many cases had, before this, been abandoned by the roadside, was now in position despite the hilly nature of the country and the hostility of the English ambassador. The exertions of preparation were most exhausting, and the near prospects of famine caused the frequent recurrence of treachery.

Hard upon this came the order from the Civil Governor of Kars that General Williams must not be obeyed as he was a "Giaour." The Russians were now in the vicinity of the city, confident of an easy conquest and of much plunder. Those deserters who escaped the bullets of the troops made the Russians aware of the condition of the garrison.

The celebrated general, Mouravieff, commanded the attacking army, which was large and perfectly equipped. He was not only a skilful, but an experienced soldier, who had served in the army which took Kars in 1828.

General Williams called a council-of-war. He summoned his lieutenants Kmety, Teesdale, Lake, Kollman and Thompson. The Civil Governor was compelled to attend. The further fortification of the city was at once determined on. Day and night, without pause, the work was carried on and the general superintended it with the utmost vigilance and care. Frequent appeals were made to the English ambassador. Sixty-four dispatches in all were sent, but to no purpose. They were not even acknowledged. Jealousy and hatred had deafened Lord Stratford to all the appeals of these heroic men and obscured the perception even of his own interests.

Food for both man and beast was running short. Sorties were made to gather forage for the horses, but it was bought with many gallant lives. In many instances the poor animals, worn to skeletons, were turned adrift upon the plain.

The state of affairs at this time is best described in a letter from General Williams to the Earl of Clarendon, dated Sept. 30th, giving a report of a sortie which he had made when, after a sharp battle of eight hours duration, the superior force of the enemy was compelled to retire to the lines of entrenchment.

"My Lord,—We could not get the messenger out of the lines last night. To-day we have repaired our breastworks, filled the tumbrils, and replenished the pouches of the infantry. so that everything as well as everybody is ready for the Russians should they wish to try their fortunes once more. We have collected and are now burying the dead—at least three thousand round the scene of especial danger, and in all the camps they have been firing volleys over those they took away and were slain at some distance by roundshot. The number of wounded cannot be less than 4,000. If we had only possessed a few hundred cavalry we should have utterly destroyed their army. Their loss in officers has been enormous, and they behaved splendidly. Three men were killed on the platform of the gun in Tackma-Tabia, which, at that moment, was worked by Major Teesdale, who then sprang out and led two charges with the bayonet. The Turks fight like heroes. Col. Lake retook the English Tabia with the bayonet, too, and Colonel

Thompson crushed them with his guns from Arab-Tabia. Such was the deadly fire of our riflemen that 2000 dead bodies now lie in front of an epaulement defended by 400 of that arm. I am so fatigued that I can scarcely hold my pen, but I am sure your lordship will pardon the scrawl.

"(Sgd.) W. F. WILLIAMS."

It will be observed that the General does not mention the part he took in that day's battle. By the prophetic vision of the pious Turks, he was of little avail, however, for they clearly saw a great host of men clothed in the green uniform of the Prophet, fighting on their side. But Dr. Sandwith says that General Williams commanded the whole of the operations of that day.

Up to the early part of October, 6,300 Russians had been interred by the garrison.

The few horses that remained were killed for food. On the 28th day of November, one hundred men died in the hospitals from starvation.

The report of the General to the Home authorities had its effect. Supplies and reinforcements were sent, but they never reached the garrison. Omar Pasha, who was entrusted with them, landed at Trebizond. This was a fatal mistake. The most ordinary military foresight, the critics maintained, would have suggested a landing at Kaleh. Had this been done, without doubt Kars would have been saved. As it was, Omar Pasha could render it no assistance.

In the month of August General Williams had warned the ambassador and the Home Office that he had provisions for but three weeks. Designed delay on the part of Lord Stratford, and his false reports to the Foreign Secretary, misled the Executive, and the men of Kars were betrayed. On December 8, 1854, he had written Lord Stratford complaining bitterly. "Having," he writes, "made this appeal to your Lordship in the name of Her Majesty's Government, it is my duty to state distinctly that I shall not be able to give such intelligence to my superiors as is absolutely necessary for them to be masters of; that I shall fail to preserve the power which I have (unaided) seized, and that I consequently shall not succeed in shielding the troops from starvation without my demands are complied with. If they be not, the dissolution of this army and the fall of Asia Minor will inevitably follow, and a golden opportunity be lost."

"No time," he said, in writing to Lord Clarendon and to the ambassador, "is to be lost; winter is gliding away from us, and our disciplined and intelligent enemy is as fully aware as I am of the destitute and disorganized state of the army which lies opposite to him."

On Nov. 19, Consul Brant apprised Lord Stratford of the note he had received from Col. Williams, as he then was, and he adds (writing to Erzeroum), "I ask from your Excellency is the Kars army to be allowed to perish? Is nothing to be done to relieve it? . . . . I now fear it must surrender, and to confer honors on its gallant defenders, while they are left to perish, is a cruel mockery and an indelible disgrace to the Turkish Government as well as to those of the Allied Powers."

Such had been the implorings that had remained unanswered. To surrender was all that could be done.

The news of his elevation to the rank of major-general coming at this time, and of his knighthood, was grim irony to the brave soldier. To the Russian general the British commander gave up his sword, on the 14th day of November. But the Russian felt such admiration for General Williams and the heroic garrison, that to each officer he gave back his sword in recognition, as he said, "of noble and devoted courage, as a mark of honour and respect."

The English general and his staff were removed to St. Petersburg and to Moscow, and were from the first moment of surrender treated with the greatest admiration and regard.

They returned to England in the spring of 1856, and were welcomed by the nation. "After having been honored," says a great paper, "by the sovereigns, the higher circles and the populations of countries for which he did not fight, and in a special manner by those of the country which he fought against, General Williams has, at length, returned to his own land in whose cause he displayed his noble qualities, whose commission he bore, and whose name he so brilliantly maintained in the face of a very energetic, capable and powerful enemy, amidst trials and difficulties unsurpassed."

On landing at Dover, he was presented with an address and was welcomed, as well as his brave officers, with the greatest enthusiasm.

On his arrival in London he was greeted with a "triumph" by the great city.

Her Majesty was pleased to confer upon him, at Buckingham Palace, the order of Knighthood of the Bath for his bravery at Kars. At the investiture, General Williams knelt before the Queen, who, in person, bade him rise. Her Majesty, assisted by His Royal Highness Prince Albert, passed round the neck of Sir William Fenwick Williams the ribbon with the badge suspended, of a "Knight Commander (military division) of the Bath."

The Queen then placed the "Star" upon his breast, and Sir William having kissed the hand of Her Majesty, withdrew. To do further honour to him, Her Majesty commanded him to sit to Mr. Mayall, the artist, in the dress worn by him at Kars.

As a still further reward, he was raised to the dignity of a baronetcy as "Sir William Fenwick Williams, of Kars." This was one of the three hereditary honours conferred upon those engaged in the Russian war. To this, by royal instance, was added an annual pension of £1,000.

His native province awaited anxiously the moment when he could pause to receive from it the "Sword of Honour" which he had proudly won and which it as proudly gave.

The ceremony is described in the *Illustrated London News* as follows : " Sword-giving, an ancient and honorable custom rewarding valour by its own peculiar weapon of defence, is not confined to the British Isles. . . . . This time we have to chronicle the gift from another quarter of the globe, Nova Scotia, a land which would appear to be doing something towards becoming celebrated, since it is the birth-place of two notorieties, one of the gown, another of the sword, both of whom have achieved world-wide reputations.

" These are 'Sam Slick' (Mr. Haliburton) and Gen. Williams, of Kars. The blade of the sword is of Nova

Scotia steel, as the simple inscription tells us, 'The Legislature of Nova Scotia presents this blade, formed of native steel, to her distinguished son, Sir William Fenwick Williams, of Kars, 1856.'

"But the blade is not the only remarkable portion. The scabbard is a work in the highest style of art, one of which Cellini might be proud. On the hilt, which is richly ornamented and gilt, are two beautiful figures of Truth and Wisdom, around which the Mayflower (the emblem of his native land), the Vine and Palm entwine; on the guard is the cipher of the General. The scabbard, which is gilt, is relieved at intervals with oxydized silver, in compartments which contain the arms of Nova Scotia, of Turkey, of Great Britain, and various trophies emblematical of Fame and Justice, with figures of Valour and Victory. These latter are the work of M. Vechte, and are very beautiful. The whole is a pleasing instance of Art decorating Victory." This was a gift which, General Williams said, touched his feelings more than all the other honors lavished upon him.

With other Crimean officers, he was banquetted at Portsmouth, where the Chivalry of England united in their praises.

He was asked to lay the foundation stone of the Memorial Chapel at Harrow School. A most distinguished company of the great men of England greeted him. The scene, upon his entry, was one of the greatest enthusiasm.

The Rev. Dr. Vaughan proposed the toast, "General Williams, of Kars," who, he said, "had done him the honour to be present."

On being introduced by Lord Palmerston, who was chairman, General Williams addressed them, saying, "My lords, ladies and gentlemen:—Dr. Vaughan asked me to come down here. I wrote back accepting the invitation, and saying that I hoped I should not be doing wrong in bringing with me some of the men of Kars. (Cheers.) In the first place, here is Colonel Lake, a Harrow man (cheers), an officer who did his duty day and night (applause). Again, here is Captain Teesdale, my A.D.C., who distinguished himself in every instance during the siege, and, on the memorable 14th of September, he kept the key of the position for fourteen hours (applause)."

At this time he was made Commander at Woolwich His arrival there was made the occasion of a grand dinner in his honour. There were present the Duke of Cambridge and many distinguished noblemen, as well as a large number of naval and military celebrities.

Lord John Russell, in the course of his remarks, paid a high tribute to the Turkish soldiers and said,

" I trust that in any future contest they may be headed by chiefs like General Williams, who will teach them the true way to maintain the independence and integrity of their country."

The University of Oxford bestowed upon him the degree of D.C.L., and he was presented with the freedom of the City of London.

" Of all the gallant men whom England has sent forth to fight her battles in the late war, no one, perhaps, has shown such capacity for command, such forethought in council, such constancy in the midst of difficulties, as General Williams." *

There is no doubt that the Home Government was aware of the neglect shown by their ambassador at Constantinople, but the mighty conflict in the Crimea had overtaxed its powers and excuses were not wanting to Lord Stratford. It must be laid to a badly arranged base of supplies and general mismanagement that no aid was sent to Kars. When he found that the fall of the city had not crushed General Williams but had won him the applause of the nation, Lord Stratford saw that it was time to change his manner of proceeding. He joined at once, loudly, in the general acclaim, but his insincerity disgusted the people

The *Naval and Military Gazette* of that date has the

---

* *Naval and Military Gazette.*

following amongst its many words of highest commendation : " The defence of Kars—more glorious in its heroic achievements, though less fortunate in its result than that of Silistria—will stand out on the page of History as the most memorable episode in the annals of the late war, and will convince the most sceptical inquirer that the race of British generals is not extinct."

So great was the general enthusiasm over the men of Kars that the arrival of Major-General Wyndham, " the hero of the Redan," was so quietly though cordially observed, that the newspapers of the time made apologies to him. General Williams was, in art, avenged by the intensity of public opinion, and the *Times* of this period is most interesting reading, as it pours the ponderous weight of its invective upon the head of Lord Stratford de Redcliffe.

During General Williams's period of service in Asiatic Turkey, he was appealed to for protection and assistance by people of many different nations. On behalf of the United States, the *Boston Courier* thanked him for his kindness and aid to Americans in Armenia, and further, took the opportunity to say that "with all his honours it is his marked distinction that he is an unostentatious, Christian gentleman." A portrait painted of him at this time shows him at his best

The accompanying cut is from it. He was of fine and pleasing presence. The expression of his face was at once fearless and gentle, combining a lofty courage, with much kindness of heart. His head was of the full, round and massive type.

Like that of so many distinguished men, his manner was quiet and unassuming, so that the resolution and capacity shown by him came in the nature of a surprise.

He was a sincere friend of his native country, and was deeply imbued with the spirit of hope for the destiny of Canada. At a public dinner in Canada, given in his honor, the unbounded cordiality of his greeting drew forth an admirable acknowledgment, part of which is as follows: . . . "The president has alluded to my services. Placed in a position of very great difficulty, I endeavored to do my duty. It has often, I thank God, fallen to my lot to reply to this toast in the old countries. I said then, as I say now I could never have performed that duty and fulfilled that trust without the concurrence of one of the bravest armies that ever handled arms. There were only four Europeans in that Turkish army. They were opposed to one of the finest armies ever sent forth by Russia. I could call it an army of polished steel. Nothing could exceed the precision of their manœu-

The Birthplace of Major-Gen. Sir W. F. Williams, of Kars, Bart.

vres. And then you must remember what a general we had against us, my dear friend, General Mouravieff—give him a cheer for my sake. (Cheers.)

You will allow me to tell you that from the moment I entered his camp up to the present we have remained in the bands of the strictest friendship. Last summer he was travelling in Italy, and regularly corresponded with me. You will understand his character when I tell you that he then sent me a sword he had had manufactured for me in the Cancasus after the siege, " and," said he, "to make it more acceptable to you I have worn it myself for six months." I must again endeavour to present to you the pleasure I feel in sitting down with you this evening and meeting your brother colonists. I was on the point of passing this, but I remembered my promise to my old and gallant friend, Sir Allan McNab, to call and see him if ever I came this way, or put foot on Canadian soil. I said I was just come to see him and must go away the next morning, but he said "no," and you all know his powers in these countries—it was impossible. Of course I bowed to impossibility, and here I am. Never did I spend a more agreeable evening, and I never shall. I have now to ask you in your turn to fill to a toast I am about to propose—one which I give in all sincerity from all my heart—" Prosperity to

Canada." Were I to talk to you, gentlemen, of the grandeur of this country, only a small corner of which I have seen ; if I were to foreshadow the future greatness of this region, which no one can think of without pride, satisfaction and the fondest hope, I should detain you for hours. I will therefore only express my hope and prayer that this country may go on prospering as it has recently done, and that it may realize the hopes not only of its own sons, but of the whole British Empire. I hope all the provinces will live and thrive like brothers, and that some, even of us, may see the day when this vast country, nine-tenths of which is still a wilderness, will be smiling fields— 'Prosperity to Canada.'"

On the 2nd of August, 1868, be became a " General of the Army." For six years he was general officer in command of the forces of British North America, during which period he administered the duties of the office with his characteristic diligence and care.

His native province was further honoured in his appointment as Lieutenant-Governor of Nova Scotia. This position he held for three years with the greatest acceptability to the people.

Subsequently, he was made Governor and Commander-in-chief at Gibraltar. This appointment lasted six years. He then occupied the honorary position ef

Constable of the Tower of London and Custos Rotulorum of the Tower Hamlets.

In the House of Lords, the Earl of Malmesbury, referring to the death of Captain Thompson, one of General Williams's lieutenants, said that his mother was in need of aid, and asked what the House thought fit to do regarding it. The Marquess of Lansdowne, in reply, said: "My noble friend has done justice on this sad occasion to the merits of that eminent man, General Williams, who has, under the peculiar circumstances in which he was placed, had the good fortune, the glory I may say, to found a military school. (Applause.)"

General Williams was twice chosen by the Liberals of Caine to represent them in the House of Commons. He wished, however, to retire from political life, and declined the re-nomination. This renowned soldier died on the 26th of July, 1883, having been in active service forty-four and one-half years.

Medals and Decorations.

1. Turkish medal and clasp for Kars.
2. Knight Commander of the Bath.
3. Grand Cross of the Legion of Honor.
4. Medjidie of the 1st Class.
5. Grand Cross of the Bath.
6. Rank of "Mushir" from the Sultan.

MAJOR-GENERAL SIR JOHN EARDLEY WILMOT INGLIS, K.C.B.

JOHN EARDLEY WILMOT INGLIS was born in the city of Halifax, in the Province of Nova Scotia, in Canada. His father was Bishop of Nova Scotia, as his grandfather had been also. He was educated at Windsor, in that province, and entered H. M. 32nd Regiment of Foot on the 2nd of August, 1833.

The first active service in which he was engaged was in the Canadian rebellion of 1837, and his first experience was at St. Denis, in the Province of Quebec. Here the British troops and Canadian loyalists, under General Gore, were defeated by the rebels; but this reverse was very soon avenged. At St. Eustache the rebel cause came to an inglorious end. Dr. Chénier, and Girod, a Swiss immigrant, had brought a roaming band together which they garrisoned in a convent. Sir John Colborne attacked them with two thousand men and the 32nd retrieved its fallen fortunes.

The troops were now able to turn their attention against St. Benoite, which they destroyed. Eleven

Major-Gen. Sir J. E. W. Inglis, K.C.B.

hundred men then set out for St. Denis, where they wreaked a summary vengeance.

The scene of the future exploits of Inglis and the 32nd Regiment was now changed to India, whither they went in 1846. He had become by meritorious service lieutenant in 1839, captain in 1843, major in 1848, and in 1855, lieut.-colonel of the 32nd Foot.

As major, Inglis served throughout the Punjaub campaign of 1848-9.

On the 18th of April, 1848, whilst a change of governors was being effected at Moultan, two British officers were treacherously killed. Ex-Dewan Moolray seized this as a favorable opportunity for beginning a Holy War of Sikhs, Mussulmans and Hindoos. In the first encounter, however, he was defeated, and he fled in retreat to Moultan, which he prepared to defend.

General Whish, with six thousand men, including the two British regiments, the 10th and 32nd, at once moved on Moultan and demanded its surrender, but before the siege-operations were made effective and the investment completed, the desertion of native troops rendered the retirement of Gen. Whish's division a necessity.

After further deliberation, another advance against Moultan was made, but this also was unsuccessful.

Finally, Lord Gough with the Army of the Punjaub, Gen. Whish having command of the first division, began the siege in a more formidable way, and on the 2nd of January, 1849, Moultan fell. The loss was very heavy.

In General Whish's report the following occurs: "On the 12th of September last, after Lt.-Col. Pattoun was mortally wounded, the command of the six companies of H. M. 32nd regiment devolved on Major Inglis, and through the exertions of the gallant troops employed, the enemy's strong position was carried."

Major Inglis took part also in the attack that resulted in the surrender of the fort and garrison of Cheniote, and he was in the subsequent battle of Goojerat. By the fall of Moultan, General Whish was enabled to form a junction with Lord Gough.

In a letter to the Adjutant-General of the army from the camp at Goojerat, Feb. 22, 1849, Major-General Whish says, "Having but recently had my attention drawn to the circumstances I am about to mention, I think in justice to the gallant officer affected by them I may be permitted to do so, though they may refer to anterior conflicts with the enemy. . . . . On the 7th of November last, when Lieut.-Col. Brooke having command of one of the two columns of attack, that of H. M. 32nd regiment again devolved on Major

Inglis, whose conduct in that important trust was highly satisfactory to the Brigadier commanding, and I have accordingly great satisfaction in soliciting the favourable notice of His Excellency to the same.

(Sig'd.) W. S. WHISH,
Major-General.

The battle of Goojerat was fought on the 22nd of February, 1849, and was remarkable chiefly for scenic display. The day was perfect. The plain was clothed with standing grain as far as the eye could reach, glinting in the sun, and the wall of the horizon was formed by the huge ramparts of the snowy range of Cashmere.

Far on the left rose the towers of the city of Goojerat, which was surrounded by ancient villages and monuments of antiquity.

The Sikhs numbered 60,000 men. At the first charge of the cavalry the enemy was driven back, and in a short time the field was won. After this battle the Kalsa army laid down its arms.

From May, 1848, to May, 1849, the utmost anxiety had prevailed, for the consequences of the war were of the utmost importance to the British Empire. The constant disappointments were terminated at Moultan and the end wrought at Goojerat.

For his services in these actions, Major Inglis received the brevet rank of lieut.-colonel and a medal with clasps, on the 5th of June, 1855.

Thus far Colonel Inglis had shown that he was a good soldier, and had attracted some attention as a brave and capable officer, but his fame was to be won at Lucknow.

The suddenness of the outbreak of the Indian Mutiny and its subsequent horrors are too well known to require more than an incidental reference.

The city of Lucknow is situated on the south-west side of the Goomtee river, which is navigable to the Ganges. Formerly the river was spanned by a bridge of boats, a large one of stone and an iron structure as well. The city extended for a distance of four miles along the river-bank. The middle portion of it dated to remote antiquity. With few exceptions, the houses were of mud, with thatched roofs. These exceptions were, however, magnificent specimens of the oriental style of architecture.

An extraordinary effect was produced by the level of the streets being ten feet or more below that of the shops, giving the city the appearance of being cut up by a net-work of canals. The streets were also exceedingly narrow. Great numbers of elephants were kept by the king and the aristocracy, and when these animals passed along these narrow defiles they filled them completely so that foot-passengers sought refuge in shops or by climbing up the stairs.

On a lofty eminence was the Stronghold of Lucknow, which was of more modern design than its predecessor.

In the part of the city called Farabaksch were numerous arcades and a few streets of some pretensions. On the right bank of the Goomtee was the Palace of the King. It was almost as luxurious as the Moorish Alhambra, having fountains of fantastic design, baths of the Roman type and terraces of the most elaborate conception.

And this palace was not without its dungeons. The lower rooms were hung with ghastly tapestry with skeletons figured in. In them were kept instruments of torture which were used to punish the inmates of the harem.

The city was famous for its Zoological Gardens. In the north-west quarter was the Imambarat, celebrated as being a perfect specimen of the florid style.

The British Residency was near the palace, and about four miles from the British cantonment. It was most inadequately garrisoned by one company. In a place of three hundred thousand of a population this was manifestly insufficient to cope with any serious disturbance.

The religions were those of the Mussulmans and Hindoos. Men of every class went fully armed, "even those at the shop-doors being equipped with shield and sword."

The minds of the people had been prepared for discontent by the unfortunate mistakes of British diplomatists.

When the mutiny and its ghastly horrors began, it seemed altogether probable that the British power in India would be extinguished in blood. Although warnings had been given they were unheeded and all in a moment the life-and-death-struggle began.

Within Lucknow, where the regiments were quartered, every preparation possible was made for defence, though many people, possessed of some altogether unaccountable idea, were determined that nothing should be done, and did nothing accordingly, to assist in making ready for attack.

Brigadier Inglis had foreseen, to some extent, the desperate nature of the coming siege. Fully realizing the unprepared state and bad position of the city, he strove with all speed to put it in condition for the struggle.

Sir Henry Lawrence, like Inglis, was a deeply religious man and refrained from touching with the profane hand of war the sacred temples of the outer city. This, in the end, required the retreat of the garrison within the Residency.

There was no time for a leisurely execution of a scientific plan of fortification, yet at no time was the defenders' courage that of despair. The grim horror of fanaticism and massacre hung over them—they thought not of that but they trembled for the women and children and well they might.

The account of the state of Lucknow during the siege, contained in the report of Brigadier Inglis, is a simple record of events of night and day—of attacks being desperately repulsed, of mines and counter-mines and of the lust and fury of fiends who had no fear.

On the 18th of June, in the evening, the force was paraded a second time and minutely inspected by Col. Inglis. He had been detailed to examine the defences and inspect the troops, in order to prepare them for the trials to come. He laboured untiringly to put them in the best possible condition. Deaths by disease and starvation had become of hourly happening. and the physical state of the garrison was at its worst, On the 4th of July the great Lawrence died. A greater misfortune could scarcely have come upon them. The following report speaks for itself:

"Brigadier Inglis, commanding the garrison of Lucknow, to the Secretary of Government, Military Department, Calcutta :

"LUCKNOW, Sept. 6, 1857.

"SIR, — In consequence of the deeply lamented death of Brigadier-General Sir Henry M. Lawrence, K.C.B., late in command of the Oude field-force, the duty of communicating the military events which have occurred at Lucknow since the 29th of June last has devolved upon myself.

" On the evening of that day several reports reached Sir Henry Lawrence that the rebel army in no very inconsiderable force would march from Chinut (a small village eight miles distant, on the road to Fyzabad) on Lucknow, on the following morning, and the late Brigadier-General therefore determined to make a strong reconnaissance in that direction with a view to the possibility of meeting the force at a disadvantage either on entering the city or at the bridge across the Gokral, which is a small stream intersecting the Fyzabad road about half way between Lucknow and Chinut. . . . The troops, misled by the reports of the wayfarers, . . . proceeded somewhat further than had been originally intended, and suddenly fell in with the enemy, who up to that time had eluded the vigilance of the advance-guard by concealing themselves behind a long line of trees, in overwhelming numbers. . . . . And had the Oude artillery been faithful and the Sikh cavalry shown a better front, the day would have been won in spite of the immense disparity in numbers. But the Oude artillerymen and drivers were traitors. They overturned the guns into the ditches, cut the traces of their horses and abandoned them, regardless of the remonstrances and exertions of their own officers and those of Sir Henry Lawrence's staff, headed by the Brigadier-General himself in person, who drew his sword on the rebels. Every effort to induce them to stand having proved ineffective, the force, exposed to the vastly superior fire of artillery and completely outflanked on both sides by an overpowering body of infantry and cavalry which actually got in our rear, was compelled to retire with a loss of three pieces of artillery which fell into the hands of the enemy in consequence of the rank treachery of the Oude gunners, and with a very grievous list of killed and wounded.

"The heat was frightful. The gun-ammunition was expended, and the almost total want of cavalry to protect the rear made our retreat most disastrous. All the officers behaved well. . . . . Sir Henry Lawrence subsequently conveyed his thanks to myself, who had at his request accompanied him upon this occasion. . . . .

(Here follow the deeds of valor of the other officers, etc.)

"It remains to report the siege-operations. . . . The untoward event of the 30th of June, so far diminished the whole available force that we had not a sufficient number of men remaining to occupy both positions. The Brigadier-General, therefore, on the evening of the 1st of July, signalled to the garrison of Muchee Bhowun to evacuate and blow up that fortress in the course of the night. The orders were ably carried out, and at 12 the force marched into the Residency with their guns and treasure, without the loss of a man and, shortly afterwards, the explosion of two hundred and forty barrels of gunpowder and six million ball-cartridges which were lying in the magazine, announced to Sir Henry and his officers, who were anxiously awaiting the report, the complete destruction of that post and all it contained. . . . It is now my very painful duty to relate the calamity which befell us at the commencement of the siege. On the first of July, an 8-inch shell burst in the room in the Residency in which Sir Henry was sitting. · .

"The whole of his staff implored Sir Henry to take up other quarters in the Residency, which had become the special target for the round shot and shell of the enemy. This, Sir Henry jestingly declined to do, observing that another shell would certainly never be pitched into that small room. But Providence had ordered otherwise, for on the very next day he was mortally wounded by a fragment of another shell which burst in the same room, exactly at the same spot. The late lamented Sir Henry Lawrence, knowing that his last hour was rapidly approaching, directed me to assume command of the troops, and appointed Major Banks to succeed him in the office of Chief-Commissioner. He lingered in great agony till the 4th of July, when he expired, and the Government was thereby deprived, if I may venture to say so, of the services of a distinguished statesman and a most gallant soldier. (He continues to speak of his winning manner and kind and pleasing disposition.) . . . The successful defence of the position has been, under Providence, solely attributable to the foresight he evinced in the timely commencement of the necessary operations and the great skill and untiring personal activity which he exhibited in carrying them into effect. . . . In him every good and deserving soldier lost a friend and a chief capable of discriminating, and ever on the alert to reward merit, no matter how humble the sphere in which it was exhibited. . . .

"Major Banks received a ball in the head while examining a critical outpost on the 21st of July, and died without a groan. . . . . When the blockade commenced only two of our batteries were completed. Part of the defences were yet in an unfinished condition, and the buildings in the immediate vicinity which gave cover to the enemy, were only very partially cleared away. (This was due to the reverence for the high places, of Sir Henry Lawrence.) . . . As soon as the enemy had thoroughly completed the investment of the Residency, they occupied these houses, some of which were within easy pistol-shot of our barricades, in immense force, and rapidly made loop-holes on those sides which bore on our post, from which they kept up a terrific and incessant fire, day and night, which caused many daily casualties, as there could not have been less than 8,000 men firing at one time into our position. Moreover, there was no place in the whole of our works that could be considered safe, for several of the sick and wounded who were lying in the banquet-hall, which had been turned into an hospital, were killed in the very centre of the building, and the widow of Lieut. Dorin and other women and children were shot dead in rooms in which it had not been deemed possible a bullet could penetrate. . . . . They soon had 20 to 25 guns in position, some of them of very large calibre. They were planted all around our post, at small distances. some being actually within 50 yards of our defences, but in places our heavy guns could not reply to them, while the perseverance and ingenuity of the enemy in erecting barricades around and in front of their guns, in a very short time rendered all attempts to silence them, by musketry, unavailing. Nor could they be effectually silenced by shells by reason of their extreme proximity to our position, and because, moreover, the enemy had recourse to digging very narrow trenches about 8 feet in depth, in rear of each gun, in which the men lay while our shells were flying, and which so effectually concealed them, even while working the guns, that our baffled sharp-shooters could only see their hands while in the act of loading. The enemy contented themselves with keeping up this incessant fire of cannon and musketry until the 20th of July, on which day at 10 a.m. they assembled in very great force all around our position and exploded a heavy mine inside our outer line of defences at the water-gate. . . . . But they were driven back with great slaughter. . . . Matters proceeded in this way till the 10th of August, when the enemy made another assault, having previously sprung a mine. . . . They beat a speedy retreat, leaving the more adventurous of their numbers lying on the crest of the breach. . At Capt. Anderson's post they also came boldly forward with scaling ladders, but here as elsewhere they were met with the most indomitable resolution. On the 18th of August the enemy sprung another mine with very fatal effect in front of the Sikh lines. Capt. Orr, unattached, and Lieuts. Meacham and Sappit, each commanding a small body of drummers, comprising the garrison, were blown into the air, but providentially returned to earth with no further injury than a severe shaking. . . . But they succeeded under cover of the breach in establishing themselves in one of the houses in our position, from which they were driven in the evening by the bayonets of H. M. 32nd and 34th foot. On the 5th of September the enemy made their last serious assault, having exploded a large mine a few feet short of the bastion of the 18-pounder in Major Apthorp's post. They advanced with large, heavy scaling ladders which they planted against the wall and mounted, thereby gaining for an instant the embrasure of the gun. They were very speedily driven back. . . . . However, a few minutes subsequently they sprung another mine close to the brigade mess and advanced boldly, but soon the corpses strewn in the garden in front of the post bore testimony to the fatal accuracy of the rifle and musketry fire of the gallant members of that garrison, and the enemy fled ignominiously, leaving their leader, a fine-looking old native-officer, among the slain. . . At other posts they made similar attacks . . . . with the same want of success. . . . . The above is a faint attempt at a description of the four great struggles which have occurred during the protracted season of exertion, exposure and suffering. . . . . But by counter-mining in all directions we succeeded in destroying no less than four of the enemy's subterraneous advances towards our position. . . . . The labor, however, which devolved upon us in making these counter mines in the absence of a body of skilled miners was very heavy. . . . . But I can conscientiously declare that few troops have undergone greater hardships, exposed as they have been to the never-ceasing musketry-fire and cannonade. They have also experienced the vicissitudes of extreme wet and intense heat . . . . in many places with no shelter at all. In addition to having had to repel real attacks, they have been exposed night and day to the hardly less harassing false alarms which the enemy have been constantly raising. The insurgents have frequently fired very heavily, sounded the advance and shouted for several hours together, though not a man could be seen, with a view of course of harassing our small and exhausted force, an object they succeeded in, for no part has been strong enough to allow of a portion only of the garrison being spared in the event of a false attack being turned into a real one. All therefore had to stand to their arms and to remain at their posts until the demonstration had ceased, and such attacks were of almost nightly occurrence. The whole of the officers and men have been on duty night and day during the eighty-seven days which the siege had lasted up to the arrival of Sir J. Outram, G.C.B. In addition to this incessant military duty the force has been nightly employed in repairing, etc. . . . During the early part of these vicissitudes we were left without any information whatever regarding the posture of affairs outside. An occasional spy did indeed come in. . . . We sent our messengers daily calling for aid and asking for information, none of whom ever returned until the 26th day of the siege, when a pensioner named Ungud came back with a letter from General Havelock's camp, informing us that they were advancing with a force sufficient to bear down all opposition, and would be with us in five or six days. A messenger was immediately despatched, requesting that on the evening of their arrival in the outskirts of the city two rockets might be sent up in order that we might take the necessary measures for assisting them while forcing their way in. The sixth day, however, expired, and they came not, but for many evenings after, officers and men watched for the ascension of the expected rockets with hopes such as make the heart sick. . . . Thirty-five days later it was learned that the relieving force, after having fought most nobly, had been obliged to fall back for reinforcements, and this was the last communication we received until two days before the arrival of Sir J. Outram, on the 25th September. Besides heavy visitations of cholera and small-pox, we have had also to contend against a sickness which has almost universally pervaded the garrison. . . . * I cannot refrain from bringing to the prominent notice of His Lordship in Council the patience, endurance and great resignation which have been evinced by the women of this garrison. They have animated us by their example. (He then gives a long list of those who merited mention). . . . In short, at last the number of European gunners was only 24, while we had, including mortars, no less than 30 guns in position. . . . With respect to the native troops, I am of opinion that their loyalty has never been surpassed. . . . We are also repaid for much suffering and privation by the sympathy which our brave deliverers say our perilous and unfortunate position has excited for us in the hearts of our countrymen throughout the length and breadth of Her Majesty's dominions.

" I have, etc., etc.,
"(Sgd.) J. INGLIS,
" Col. H. M. 32nd,
" *Brigadier.*"

On the 19th of September Havelock and Outram passed the Ganges, and by the 25th had forced their way to the relief of Lucknow, not one hour too soon, as the Residency had been mined and the provisions of the garrison were nearly exhausted. The British force was obliged to cut its way through the disaffected city of Lucknow before it could reach the Residency, and as it approached the British entrenchments an enthusiastic excitement was displayed which has but few parallels in history. The pent-up feelings and anxious suspense of the garrison gave way in a burst of deafening cheers.

On the 22nd spies had come in with rumors of the approach of Generals Havelock and Outram. The bare thought of their truth excited the most longing hope in the breasts of the besieged. Many had died from the exhaustion of fatigue.

On the 25th their anxiety was relieved, for at some distance off they could hear the loud thunder of artillery, and to the excitement was added the rage of renewed ardor of battle. A day of suspense followed. Then the firing began again and nearer the city.

The insurgents were put to flight, and " at last a loud shout proclaimed the arrival of the long-expected reinforcements. The immense enthusiasm with which they were greeted defies description. As their hurrah and ours rang in my ears I was nigh bursting with joy. The tears started involuntarily into my eyes, and I felt—no! It is impossible to describe in words that sudden sentiment of relief, that mingled feeling of hope and pleasure that came over me. . . . . . We felt not only happy, happy beyond imagination, . . . but we also felt proud of the defence we had made. . . . ."

Without distinction, for it was no time for that, without the least shadow of formality, officers and men silently shook each others hands, and with tears falling, embraced their comrades who had been snatched from a fearful death. "And these brave men themselves, many of them bleeding and exhausted, forgot the loss of their comrades, the pain of their wounds, the fatigue of overcoming the fearful obstacles they had combatted for our sakes, in the pleasure of having accomplished our relief." Nor shall the chivalrous conduct of some of the Sepoys ever be forgotten.

In reference to the siege of Lucknow, the *Times* says: "The defence of that place is, we believe, without precedent in modern warfare. . . . But neither Genoa nor Saragossa can rival in heroism the little Residency of Lucknow."

In the *Naval and Military Gazette* of November, 1857, is the following: "Amid the thankful rejoicings of the relieved garrison of Lucknow, and the hearty congratulations of the noble soldiers who, led by Havelock, have at last won their way to their long attempted achievement, we doubt if there is any who has felt more thankful to a guiding Providence than that devout soldier of the Cross, Havelock himself. We envy the feelings of such a man, when he rushed with his noble followers to greet the relieved garrison. It is a bright picture on which the mind dwells the more delightedly from having for so long feared to think upon Lucknow while the horrors of Cawnpore were fresh in the recollection, and agonizing every heart."

No higher tribute could be paid than that of Sir John Outram, whose reports abound with generous sentiments of admiration. Nor were the material rewards of the soldiers neglected. In the general order of the Government of India all the troops were remembered. And in the General Order of Dec. 8, 1857, of the Governor of India, is contained this passage: " There does not stand recorded in the annals of war an achievement more truly heroic than the defence of the Residency of Lucknow, ..." Two days after another order was issued dealing with the military operations, and it says, " They (the operations) are explained fully and clearly, and every sentence bears proof of their having been guided by a master-hand, and that unbounded mutual confidence between the soldiers and their commander."

There is also in the *London Gazette* of February 17th the General Order of the Governor of India in Council, containing further despatches from Major-General Havelock, K.C.B., and Major-General Outram, G.C.B.: " They (these despatches) show how thoroughly this gallant band has sustained the reputation of British soldiers for courage, discipline and determination."

Nor should an extract from the *Times* be omitted of Nov. 16, 1857, from an editorial referring to Lucknow and Delhi: " Here will be seen what was dared by and suffered by the brave men to whom we owe deliverance from one of the greatest perils that ever threatened the Empire. . . . . The country has, we all feel, repaired its renown which was for a while wounded by the episode of the Crimea. . . . . We have now shown the world that we have generals who can command, as well as soldiers, etc. . . . . The men who became notorious two or three years since may now be consigned to a contemptuous oblivion."

The arduous duties which had devolved upon Brigadier Inglis and staff had prevented him from furnishing to the Major-General commanding, at the proper time, the usual official information regarding the defence, for it must be remembered that it was not for some time that Sir Colin Campbell brought away the garrison. Without this, the Major-General, as he said, could not indulge in public praise of the heroism of Brigadier Inglis and his garrison. At last the report was made, and the Major-General expressed officially the admiration of the British people. " The Major-General believes that the annals of war contain no brighter page than that which will recall the bravery, fortitude, vigilance and patience, endurance of hardships, privations and fatigue displayed by the garrison of Lucknow." This officer continues to speak of "the incredible difficulties with which they had to contend," and further says, "For while the devoted band of heroes who so nobly maintained their country's arms under Sir Robt. Sale at Jellalabad were seldom exposed to actual attack, the Lucknow garrison, of inferior strength, have, in addition to a series of fierce assaults gallantly and successfully repulsed, been for three months exposed to a nearly incessant fire from strong and commanding positions, held by an enemy of overwhelming force, possessing powerful artillery, having at their command the whole resources of what was but recently a kingdom, and animated by an insane and bloodthirsty fanaticism."

In his famous' report of the 26th of September, 1857, to the Secretary to the Governor, Military Department, Calcutta, Inglis says, regarding his old regiment: " The losses sustained by H. M. 32nd, which is now barely 300 strong, by H. M. 84th and the artillery, show at least that they knew how to die in the cause of their countrymen."

The following extract, of a somewhat different phase, is from the preface to the " Siege of Lucknow," by R. P. Anderson, and is written by T. C. Anderson, 12th regiment, N.I., editor: "There never was such a siege as that of Lucknow, nor can history approach a parallel to it either in the extraordinary circumstances of the siege or the bravery of its garrison, including that of the women shut up there. The Spartan women of old were celebrated for having cut off their hair to make bowstrings for their husbands, but the heroism of our sisters at Lucknow surpasses any of their deeds. When we reflect upon the privations and horrors to which they were subjected, one can hardly believe that it is not from a long dream that we have been awakened. Hope was so long deferred that we had truly almost numbered the heroic little garrison with the dead. Each member of that garrison should receive the Victoria Cross.

"(Sg'd.)   T. C. ANDERSON."

The final attack of the rebels is well described in the *Illustrated London News* of the 21st of November, 1857, under the heading of "Lucknow." " No sooner had the rebels received information that Havelock was again menacing the Ganges than they determined to make a tremendous effort to overpower the garrison. They detached a large body to attack Havelock near Oonao, and with the remainder of the force attacked our people. Some of them were actually penetrating into the entrenchments when a sudden inspiration seized our men. There were plenty of shells but no mortars. Our men, reckless of life and resolved to conquer or perish, seized the shells, lighted the fuses, and taking them in their hands hurled them with all their force at the enemy. It is not easy to conquer men who would dare such an action as this, so at least the enemy thought—they fell back, awed and cowed, and did not resume the attack that day."

Havelock on arriving at Lucknow sent the 78th Highlanders on ahead into the city. Led by them, the relieving force fought with the ferocity of those who were maddened by the remembrance of Cawnpore. Discipline was for a time almost set aside, and individual men with the one fierce desire for revenge ran out of the ranks and attacked the natives. The fighting was hard, for the rebels were numerous and brave, but nothing could withstand Havelock's brigade. In regard to the truth of the story of Jessie Brown, it may be said that one party maintains its correctness whilst another denies it. The latter alleges that it came to England from a French source. Even if the latter be true, it is a fair indication of what the French narrators thought of so unusually dramatic a situation.

When the 78th were drawing near to the beleaguered city and before the garrison was aware that help had come, they began playing their bagpipes as they marched. When the first notes were borne upon the wind to the ears of the defenders, the realization of so faint a hope came like an intoxication. Amongst the sick and wounded, was one poor Scottish girl who never ceased to flit about, rendering help to the sick and wounded. At last she was attacked by fever, and her mind began to wander. She was wrapped tenderly in her Highland plaid and laid upon the ground. A lady sat beside her, promising to awaken her when, as the poor girl said, " her father should return from the ploughing." She at length fell into a profound slumber, motionless and apparently breathless, her head resting in the kind lap of her attendant, who, in turn, overcome with fatigue, soon fell asleep in spite of the continual roaring of the cannon. Suddenly Jessie rose up with a wild, unearthly scream, her arms raised and her head bent forward as if listening. A look of intense delight broke over her face, and clinging with convulsive grasp to her friend she cried, " Dinna ye hear it? Dinna ye hear it? I am no' dreaming. It is the slogan of the Highlanders. We are saved! We are saved!" Her companion thought her gone mad, but she rushed out to the men at the guns and shrieked " Courage! Hark to the slogan—to the MacGregor—the grandest o' them a'!"

It could not yet be heard by the others, till presently it reached their ears, when all was changed to sobbing and prayer. To the cheering of "God Save the Queen," the 78th replied in the plaintive song that

The Birthplace of Major-Gen. Sir J. E. W. Inglis.

moves every Scot to tears, "Should auld acquaintance be forgot."

It has been ascertained that all the facts that have been collected point to the truth of the pretty incident. From what they had escaped may be better realized when it is understood that the East Indians never give or take quarter.

For this achievement, Col. Inglis was promoted to the rank of Major-General and made a K.C.B., " for his enduring fortitude and persevering gallantry in the defence of the Residency of Lucknow for 87 days, against an overwhelming force of the enemy."

"THE FATHER OF THE ROYAL NAVY,"
SIR PROVO WILLIAM PARRY WALLIS, G.C.B.

Senior Admiral of the Fleet.

PROVO WILLIAM PARRY WALLIS was born at Halifax, in the Province of Nova Scotia, a place which, from its proximity to the ocean, has furnished many sea-faring men. This event took place on the 12th of April, 1791.

The father of the present admiral was Provo Featherstone Wallis, Esquire, Chief Clerk in the office of the Commissioner of the Navy Yard, at that port. As was common in those days, his son was sent to England for his further education. The son is still living in the year 1890.

The record of his life connects a by-gone era of the British Navy with the present time. He has witnessed a complete revolution in the construction of ships and in naval methods. In his youth, no step could be taken, no promotion gained, except, as in the poets' time, by the grace of patronage. This has happily passed away.

Sir Provo Wallis, G.C.B.,
Senior Admiral of the Fleet.

Though born in the 18th century, his memory still retains its clearness, and he could easily pass his examinations over again in the minutiæ of the naval code. But his mind has outlived his body, and he is in a very feeble state of health. How great is the regret, then, that he has not thought his deeds and experiences worthy of detailed remembrance.

"Funtington House,
"West Chichester,
"Sussex, England.
"Dec. 21st, 1888.

"To J. Hampden Burnham, Esq.

"Dear Sir,—I am sorry not to have answered your very complimentary letter sooner, but am obliged to do so when I feel equal to the task, as I am now in my 98th year, being born on the 12th April, 1791, at Halifax.

"I regret to say that I have not kept any notes of my life, and have been obliged, at this late time of day, to decline undertaking the job, though asked by many to do so, ... or should you have seen or could do so, the life of my late Capt., Sir Philip Broke, you will see rather more particulars. Excuse *more*, as I write from my bed, having done so for some time.

"I am, yours very truly,

"(Sgd.) Provo Wm. Parry Wallis."

The handwriting of this letter is wonderfully smooth and steady, quite as much so as that of a man of forty years of age.

This officer was the cotemporary of Nelson, and entered the service, with other naval celebrities, about the same time, and he is the sole survivor of that period.

According to the custom absolute, of those days, he was booked for service while yet in the nursery, but it was not till 1804, that he began his career. He was then appointed midshipman in the *Cleopatra* 32, Captain Sir Robert Laurie.

"We sailed," he says, "shortly after for the N. A. Station; and on the 16th of February, 1805, at daylight (lat. 20° N., long. 67° W.), came in sight of a ship standing to the eastward. All sail was made in chase, but it was not until ten in the morning of the 17th that she was overtaken.

"The stranger was the French 18-pounder 40-gun frigate *Ville de Milan*. At 11 h. 30 m., the latter having shortened sail and hauled to the wind, hoisted her colours, and the *Cleopatra*, having also shortened sail, fired her bow-guns and commenced a running fight. At 2 h. 30 m., the *Cleopatra* being within one hundred yards of her antagonist, the *Ville de Milan* luffed across the bows of the British ship and opened her broadside.

The *Cleopatra*, passing under her adversary's stern, returned the fire and, ranging up within musket-shot, a determined fight took place, both ships running parallel to each other, sometimes nearly before the wind and, at others, close-hauled. At 5h., having shot away the main top-sail yard of the *Ville de Milan*, the *Cleopatra* forged ahead, and her running rigging being so much cut that she could neither shorten sail nor back her maintop-sail, her captain determined to endeavour to cross the bows of the enemy. Just as the *Cleopatra* was putting her helm down for this purpose, a shot disabled her wheel.

" The French frigate, observing the ungovernable state of her antagonist, bore up and ran her on board, the bowsprit and figure-head passing over the quarter-deck, abaft the main rigging.

" From the commanding position of her adversary, owing to the strong wind and heavy sea running, the *Cleopatra* was in danger of being sunk by her heavy opponent. The French crew in their attempt to board were at first repulsed with loss, but about 5h. 15m. the overpowering numbers of the assailants overcame all opposition and the British colours were hauled down. Shortly after the *Cleopatra's* fore and mainmasts went over the side, and the bowsprit soon followed. In this desperate action the *Cleopatra* had only two hundred men at quarters, and of this number, sixteen seamen, three marines, and one boy were killed ; total, twenty-two mortally wounded or killed, and thirty-six wounded.

"Captain Renaud of the *Ville de Milan* was killed by the last shot fired from the *Cleopatra*, and her loss, though not stated, was also heavy. The *Ville de Milan* was a ship of 1,100 tons, mounted forty-six heavy guns —long 18 and 8-pounders, and had on board 350 men, whereas the *Cleopatra* measured 690 tons only and was armed with long 12-pounders and 24-pounder carronades.

"Having removed the prisoners and put on board forty-nine officers and men, the prize and the *Ville de Milan* (whose main and mizzenmasts having fallen during the night, she was, consequently, only juryrigged), continued their course homeward, but on the 23rd of February, were descried by the 50-gun ship *Leander*, Captain the Honourable John Talbot, which ship immediately chased.

"The weather coming on thick, the *Leander* lost sight of the frigates, but at 2h. 30m. again obtained a view of them. The *Ville de Milan* closed for mutual support, and having fired a gun to leeward, each hoisted a French ensign upon the mainstay. At 4h. the *Leander* arrived within gun-shot and the frigates separated, the *Cleopatra* running before the wind and the *Ville de Milan* hauling up with the wind, on the larboard quarter.

" At 4h. 30m. the *Leander* fired a shot at the *Cleopatra*, upon which the French colours were hauled down and the ship hove to.

" Those of the original crew of the *Cleopatra* who remained on board then rushed upon deck and took possession of the ship, and Captain Talbot, directing the *Cleopatra* to follow, immediately pursued the *Ville de Milan*.

" Before 6 p. m., the *Leander* having got alongside the *Ville de Milan*, that ship surrendered without firing a shot. The French ship was added to the British Navy under the name of the *Milan*, and was classed as an 18-pounder, 38-gun frigate." *

This was the young midshipman's first experience in action. His next appointment was with the *Cambrian* 38, and whilst cruising in her off the Antiguan station they heard of the battle of Trafalgar. For some time they gave themselves up to festivities in honour of the event.

Shortly after this, he was appointed to another vessel on the North American station, till November,

---

* *Three British Admirals*, by Rev. Dr. Brighton.

1806, when he was promoted to the seventy-four, the *Triumph*, under Sir Thomas Hardy, better known as "Nelson's Hardy." In 1808, he received his promotion as lieutenant, at seventeen years of age, of the *Curieux*.

This ship, however, ran ashore on the island of Petite Têne, during the blockade of Guadaloupe, and was burned by order of her captain.

He then received a lieutenancy in the *Gloire*, a much larger ship than the *Curieux*, and assisted in the destruction of the battery of Ane la Bergue and the French frigates, when the action was so desperate that the Frenchmen were not towable, and sank.

He also took part in the capture of the Island of Guadaloupe shortly afterwards, and for his services received a medal.

He served in three other men-o'-war till his appointment, in 1812, to the *Shannon*, Capt. Broke.

Capt. Broke was no ordinary officer. He had studied very carefully the laying of a ship's ordnance—that is to say, he had learned thoroughly how to give the most effective broadside.

When the *Shannon* was fitted out and put in commission he had inspected her and seen that every facility was afforded for the manipulation of the guns.

It was in the year following this that an event took

place which quite overshadowed any affair in which he had been concerned, and restored the prestige of the British flag in the western world.

It will be remembered that in 1812, a serious misunderstanding arose between Great Britain and the United States.

England had blockaded American ports and had insisted on the right to search American ships for British sailors. A remonstrance was made. The blockade was raised, but the "right of search" was still maintained.

In due course, the British minister at Washington proposed that negotiations should be opened for the restoration of peaceful relations. But the Yankees considered themselves too deeply insulted for this, and finally, much against the will of the coast-towns, war began.

Canadians remember with just pride, the beginning of this war.

The Americans attacked Canada, but at Detroit and other places were signally repulsed.

Yet on the home of the British sailor—the sea—misfortune had overtaken him. In Lake Erie, a whole fleet of British war-ships surrendered.

The struggle was carried on with much bitterness and bravery.

England had a thousand ships and the United States had twenty. Though engaged with the first Napoleon in a conflict to the death, it was thought that she had ships enough to crush the brave and independent Americans.

Disaster followed disaster. In as many weeks five British ships were taken by the Yankees, and those, chiefly by one vessel.

British dignity was confounded, and contempt gave place to anxiety on the part of the enemy. Could it be that a nation was rising to dispute Britain's sovereignty of the sea? Her enemies rejoiced and her friends were much chagrined.

In the heart of every British sailor burned fiercely the desire to wipe out every trace of these indignities. Active measures were taken. American ports were more closely blockaded. English ships sailed up and down the enemy's coast in anxious search of battle.

In the year 1812, nothing of importance occurred in the *Shannon's* cruise. In company with the *Tenedos*, a ship of similar size and armament, she stood off Chesapeake Bay, where the American *Chesapeake* and the famous *Constitution* lay. As Capt. Broke was very desirous of having a duel, ship to ship, and wishing to have no advantage on the British side, in respect of numbers, or of guns, he ordered the *Tenedos* to stand away to sea and not rejoin till the 14th of June.

On the 26th of May, the *Shannon* re-captured a Nova Scotian brig, and, a little later, another; but many prizes were destroyed. as they could not be manned.

Capt. Broke had sent several requests to the *Chesapeake,* which alone was ready for sea; but her captain had not seen fit to answer. In consequence, Capt. Broke, fearing his messages had not been received, sent a formal challenge to Capt. Lawrence, giving the fullest particulars as to the strength and equipment of the *Shannon,* and imploring him to come out.

He ended his *carte de défi.* as follows :—" I entreat you, sir, not to imagine that I am actuated by mere personal vanity to the wish of meeting the *Chesapeake,* or that I depend only on your personal ambition, for your acceding to the invitation. We have both nobler motives. You will feel it as a compliment if I say that the result of our meeting may be the most grateful service I can render to my country. And I doubt not that you, equally confident of success, will feel convinced that it is only by repeated triumphs, in even combats, that your little navy can now hope to console your country for the loss of that trade it can no longer protect. Favour me with a speedy reply.

We are short of provisions and water, and cannot stay long here."

This was never received by Capt. Lawrence. The American vessel had 376 men, and was of 1,135 tons; the *Shannon*, of 1,066 tons, and had a complement of 306 men. Taking her guns and all into account, the *Chesapeake* had the advantage.

The time at last had come. The first of June was a lovely day, worthy of the event which was to render it memorable.

Boston Bay was moved by a slight breeze that served to fill the sails of the noble ships and give the men that refreshing sense of strength which nerves to great deeds.

Now and then the two big ships heaved in the long, slow swell, and the sailors sang as they braced the yards.

The *Shannon* came easily along down the coast, and Capt. Broke looked anxiously for some movement on the part of the enemy. He knew well that "when Greek meets Greek then comes the tug o' war."

So well trained were the men aboard the British ship that they were always ready for battle.

At eight bells in the morning, second-lieutenant Wallis took the watch. The many details of cleaning the ship were gone through with in the quiet morning, and the *Shannon* kept reaching across the bay as the beat to quarters, called up her men to be put through their gun-exercises. All this the Americans could see.

Capt. Broke ascended the *Shannon's* main-top and remained there anxiously looking to see if the enemy were showing signs of coming out. But the *Chesapeake* did not move, and the *Shannon's* captain, sorely disappointed, descended, ordering the retreat from quarters, saying to the officer of the watch, " Wallis, I don't mean this for general quarters, but because she (with a gesture towards the harbor) will surely come out to-day or to-morrow."

Lieut. Falkner relieved Wallis from his watch, who, as he went below, said, " Be sure you call me if she stir."

The afternoon dragged on. The early evening waned. Still Capt. Broke lingered on deck. Suddenly the word flew along the decks—" she moves"—and every eye was strained to watch the *Chesapeake*.

What a splendid sight! With all sails spread to catch every breath of wind, the stately *Chesapeake* stood out, attended by a multitude of small boats which were filled with the people of Boston, who came out to applaud the victory of the *Chesapeake*.

Captain Lawrence, of the *Chesapeake*, was a fine specimen of manhood. He was more than ordinarily muscular, of daring and warlike spirit, and in every way fitted to lead his brave men.

Shortly before, whilst captain of the *Hornet*, he had sunk the British brig, *Peacock*, in a few minutes, by running her on board.

On this occasion he drew his men up, and appealing alike to their patriotism and their cupidity, promised them a large amount of prize-money, and closed with the words, " Peacock her, my lads, Peacock her."

No such words were spoken on board the *Shannon*. Short of provisions and stale from long cruising, there was no spirit of bravado in her crew. They were silent, like Cromwell's men, and not less confident in battle.

The British captain descended to his cabin, and, having made his final arrangements, came on deck again. The duel-ground was twenty miles from the harbor of Boston, and the vessels gradually worked up to it.

Broke, feeling that the responsibility of his position would require from him a few plain words to his men, spoke to them saying that the time had now come for which they had been awaiting to avenge the repeated disasters and insults which the nation had suffered, and that their people at home, in old England, expected that the news from over the sea would be that Britain's sons were Britons still—that they knew how to fight, as in the days when Effingham swept the main.

Capt. Broke told them also of the taunts of their enemies, the world over, that England would have to haul down her haughty flag. "Don't try to dismast her. Fire into her quarters, main-deck into main-deck, quarter-deck into quarter-deck. Kill the men and the ship is yours. Don't hit them about the head, for they have steel-caps on, but give it them through the body. Don't cheer. Go quietly to your quarters. I feel sure you will do your duty, and remember you have now the blood of hundreds of your countrymen to avenge."

The stillness on the *Shannon's* deck was intensely solemn. The captain's words had recalled vividly to the men's minds the fate of the *Macedonian*, the *Guerrière*, the *Java*, the *Peacock*, and many other victims of the prowess of the Americans.

One of the crew of the *Guerrière*, on board the *Shannon*, said, "I hope, sir, you will give us revenge for the *Guerrière* to-day."

"You shall have it, my man," said Broke, "go to your quarters."

Another innocently asked if the *Shannon* might not have as many ensigns as the *Chesapeake*, but was kindly refused his request.

Under equal sail, the ships drew near each other, the officers and men being all ready at their stations.

The main-deck was commanded by Lieuts. Wallis and Falkner. The *Chesapeake*, just as the *Hornet* had done, rounded on the starboard quarter of the *Shannon*. Captain Broke gave orders to the main-deck officers to fire on the enemy as soon as the guns bore on her second bow-port.

When the *Chesapeake* was at this point the *Shannon* began the fight, firing the main-deck gun, then, as the enemy ranged alongside, the *Shannon* delivered her broadside. The effect was terrible. Capt. Lawrence fell, mortally wounded. Many men were slain, and the air was filled with flying splinters and a cloud of dust. The *Chesapeake* had been most effectually raked.

The men of the *Chesapeake* had been ordered to rely, mainly, on their small arms. As their vessel swung round, they used them with great effect. Then the *Shannon* gave her another fearful broadside, and her crew began their musketry-fire.

The *Chesapeake* was now falling astern, and as soon as she touched the British ship, Captain Broke, raising his sword aloft, shouted, "Follow me who can!" and boarded. His men had firmly lashed the ships together.

On the decks of the *Chesapeake* a desperate conflict raged. Some of the *Shannon's* midshipmen had boarded off the fore-yard and chased their opponents down to the deck.

The *Chesapeake* had now, by reason of the rising of the wind, broken the lashings and run across the *Shannon's* bow. Captain Broke, on her forecastle, was exerting himself to save some of the enemy from the fury of his men. At this moment a sad mistake occurred. In undue haste, the first-lieutenant of the *Shannon* had run up the white ensign *under* the American flag. In an instant a shot from his own vessel blew off his head and wounded several of his comrades. Confusion followed. Trusting to this, the Americans, including those who had been spared, rushed upon Captain Broke from behind, but, turning at the shout of a sentinel, he confronted them. The odds, however, were too great. After a short struggle a pike-thrust tore away part of his skull and laid bare his brain. His men, at this, came up and almost rent the enemy in pieces. Tenderly they raised their gallant captain, streaming with blood and covered with lime which the Americans had prepared to throw in the eyes of the boarders. They bore him to the quarter-deck, and one of them crying, "Look there, sir, there goes the old ensign over the Yankee colours," he smiled faintly, in satisfaction.

A large body of the enemy had been driven below and were imprisoned, and a sentinel stood over them at the open grating. Watching their chance, the prisoners fired up and killed a man. Lieut. Falkner threatened to annihilate them if they fired again. The noise roused the *Shannon's* captain. He raised himself up and ordered that the enemy be driven into the hold, and then he fell back insensible.

Lieutenant Wallis was now in command.

In thirteen minutes the battle had been fought and won. Two hundred and fifty-two men had been placed *hors de combat,* so desperate had been the action. In the general engagement off Cape Vincent, the total loss was two hundred and ninety-six, and at Navarino, the number was two hundred and seventy-two.

Captain Broke was carried back to his own ship with the first-lieutenant of the *Chesapeake,* who had been mortally wounded. The Americans had provided handcuffs for the British, but, as Lieut. Wallis said, "with their own they were now ornamented."

The Boston pleasure-ships returned to their harbor. Throughout the long twilight the dead were "committed to the deep," as the burial-service was read over them.

Lieut. Wallis put a crew on board the *Chesapeake* and, followed by the regretful gaze of the throngs on shore, he bore away for Halifax.

On Sunday, the 6th of June, the *Shannon* and her

prize entered this port, where the enthusiasm of the people may be better imagined than pourtrayed.

"Headed by Judge Haliburton," they all rushed headlong to the landing-place, and gave the victors a more than royal welcome.

For several days the city was given up to rejoicing, then the *Shannon* was ordered to England with Commander Wallis, as he was now styled, in her, as the invited guest of Sir Philip Broke.

When the good ship reached England, her officers and crew were thanked by the Prince Regent and entertained by the City of London. Medals for the occasion were struck and distributed, and Captain Broke was created a baronet.

Lieut. Wallis in addition, received a "letter of approbation" from the Admiralty, and a sword from his captain. Of him he spoke as "a man I loved most sincerely."

It may be interesting to notice here the conclusion arrived at by the Court of Inquiry of the United States, instituted for the purpose of reporting on the cause of defeat. The decision was as follows :

" . . . . From this view of the engagement, and a careful examination of the evidence, the court are unanimously of opinion that the capture of the

United States frigate *Chesapeake* was occasioned by the following causes :—

"The almost unexampled early fall of Capt. Lawrence and all the principal officers; the bugleman's desertion of his quarters, and his inability to sound his horn, for the court are of opinion if the horn had been sounded when first ordered, the men being then at their quarters, they would have promptly repaired to the spar-deck, probably have prevented the enemy from boarding, and certainly have repelled them, and might have returned the boarding with success; and the failure of the men in both decks to rally on the spar-deck when the enemy had boarded, which might have been done successfully, it is believed, from the cautious manner in which the enemy came on board."

The strongest argument that can be adduced to confute this conclusion is the opinion of their own men.

Lieut. Ludlow, when being carried on board the *Shannon*, acknowledged that the *Shannon* " beat her fairly."

As to the charge of brutality on the part of the British, it need only be said that Lieut. Cox, of the *Chesapeake*, admitted subsequently, that his life had been spared by the forbearance of one of the *Shan-*

non's marines, and he further affirmed that the men of the *Shannon* had acted according to the best usages of war.

Commander Wallis was then appointed to the *Snipe*. Shortly after this he went out of active service on half-pay.

He was in Paris when Napoleon escaped from Elba. From this city, owing to the kindness of a dignitary high in the Roman Catholic Church, he received warning of what was about to happen, and succeeded in making his escape in safety.

Returning to England, he married a daughter of Archdeacon Barnstaple.

In a few years he re-entered active service and gained his post-rank.

He was then appointed to the *Niemen*. It was in this ship that he had command of the first experimental squadron of the fleet.

Several years subsequently he became captain of the *Madagascar*. In her he protected the British subjects at Vera Cruz when the French fleet bombarded it in the Franco-Mexican war. For his services he received the public thanks, not only of the rescued, but of the large number of British merchants whose interests had been at stake there.

In 1843 he was made captain of the *Warspite*, 50, and senior officer in the river Tagus.

He then joined the Mediterranean fleet.

In the year 1844, Tangier and Mogadar were bombarded by the French under Rear-Admiral the Prince de Joinville.

At these places he was the special envoy of England, and for the skilfulness and success of his services on these occasions he received the thanks of both the British and the French governments.

In the next year he was senior-officer on the Syrian coast, throughout the Syrian war. In 1849 he was married again, his second wife being a daughter of the late General Sir Robert Wilson, M.P.

Following this he was made an aide-de-camp to Her Majesty, preferring that honor to the good-service pension which was offered to him. In 1851 he obtained full flag-rank.

"In 1857, I was appointed commander-in-chief on the south-east coast of America and hoisted my flag on board the *Cumberland* 70, but was recalled the following year, in consequence of my promotion to vice-admiral."

Since 1858 he has not been to sea, but his services had been of such length and so peculiarly active in character that he was placed upon the "active" list for life. The rule is that admirals must retire from "active service" at the age of seventy, and their names are written thenceforth in the Navy List, in italics. The distinguished honour, therefore, which Admiral Wallis enjoys is wholly unique.

On May 18th, 1880, he was made a K.C.B., and in 1875, Admiral-of-the-Fleet. He is the senior officer in the Navy List.

" In more ways than one is Sir Provo a link between the obsolete past and the scientific present. When he entered the service, and for many years afterwards, there was no steam-navy. The first steam-vessels, and they were only tugs, did not appear in Portsmouth harbor until nearly the twenties, and Sir Provo never served in a steam-vessel of any kind; that he never served in an ironclad or even an iron ship, never was shipmates with the breech-loading gun, or indeed with a heavy gun of any sort, as heavy guns now go ; never had proving acquaintance with torpedoes and the electric light—these are assertions that can be truthfully made concerning no naval officer save Sir Provo Wallis on the active list of any service.

" He is old enough to have known and served under Lord Bridport, Lord Hood, Sir Richard Hughes, Lord Hotham, Lord St. Vincent, Lord Duncan, Cornwallis, Lord Keith, Lord Nelson, Lord Collingwood or Sir Robert Calder.

"He is modern enough to know Lord Charles Beresford, Mr. Whitehead, Mr. Beeman, Lord Armstrong and Captain Zalinski. The officer who was at the head of the Admirals' list when Sir Provo became a midshipman, was Admiral-of-the-Fleet, Sir Peter Parker, Bart., who was born in 1721, and who entered the Navy about 1735. He may well have known and served under Admiral-of-the-Fleet, Sir John Norris, who lived until 1749, and who had been promoted captain for his gallant behaviour at the battle of Beachy Head, on June 30th, 1690.

"Thus the service careers of only three officers—Wallis, Parker and Norris—are long enough to carry us directly back to the Revolution of 1688. Surely at no period of our history has any officer gained a better right than Sir Provo William Parry Wallis to be called the Father of the Royal Navy."*

* *The Times.*

ADMIRAL SIR GEORGE AUGUSTUS WESTPHAL.

GEORGE AUGUSTUS WESTPHAL was born on the 27th March, 1785, at Preston, Nova Scotia. This officer was entered in the Navy in the year 1798, under the auspices of the Duke of Kent, who had lived in Canada for a long time and was in the habit of exerting his influence in favour of Canadians. His first ship was the *Porcupine;* his period of activity dating from 1803. After serving in various stations he changed to the *Amphion*, sailing in the Mediterranean with Nelson, whom he followed into the *Victory.*

In her, after pursuing the combined fleets of France and Spain to the West Indies and back again, he fought at Trafalgar, and, being very severely wounded, was laid in the cockpit by the side of his dying chief.

Having recovered, he served in the *Ocean* 98, under Capt. Fraser, and from this he went with Lord St. Vincent into the *Caledonia* 120, when stationed off Brest. He was then, 1806, made lieutenant of the *Demarara*, a sloop in the West Indies.

Whilst on a voyage to England on the ship *Highlander*, a merchantman, as an invalid, having succumbed to the climate, his ship had the misfortune to fall in with a French man-o'-war. The *Highlander* was not in a condition to do much fighting, but Lieut. Westphal took command and fought the Frenchmen desperately for three hours. Notwithstanding this resistance, the *Highlander* was taken, and Westphal, badly wounded, confined a close prisoner. He contrived to effect his escape in an open boat, and after enduring frightful privations, and having been adrift many days, he was at last picked up by a friendly vessel.

He was then appointed to the *Neptune*, and took part again in the pursuit of a French squadron to the West Indies. He received his promotion on the 8th November to the *Belle Isle* 74, and served in her at the reduction of Martinique.

Upon his return with the prisoners of war, he was despatched to the Scheldt. During the attack upon Flushing, Lieut. Westphal, who was in command of a portion of the fleet, was under fire for fifty-two consecutive hours.

As first-lieutenant of the *Implacable* 74, in 1810, a strange adventure befell him. He sailed for Quiberon Bay with Baron De Kolli, who had undertaken to liberate Ferdinand VII. of Spain. For his services in this expedition he was to receive a post-captaincy. This, however, he did not then obtain, as the voyage was unsuccessful. He landed the Baron at night during a heavy storm, for the purpose of rescuing Ferdinand, but, notwithstanding the dangers they had escaped, an unfortunate series of accidents brought about complete failure.

The next occasion on which Westphal appears is in the defence of Cadiz, where he aided greatly in the expulsion of the French from Moguer and the adjacent coast. Of his conduct at Cadiz, Commodore Cockburn said: "I must beg leave to make mention to you (Sir Richard Goodwin Keats) of the unremitting assistance I have received from Lieut. Westphal, first of the *Implacable*, who, by his conduct and services, has added to the many claims he already had to my particular notice and recommendation."

At this period he commanded the *Implacable's* boats in many a hard fight between Rota and Puerto Santa Maria. In 1811 he sailed to Vera Cruz with two Spanish line-of-battle ships, 120, and returned with two million Spanish dollars in specie.

After Barosa, he contributed in a very important degree to the capture of the enemy's works between Catalina and Santa Maria. He was then appointed to the command of the *Alfred* 74, and was made acting-commander of the *Columbine*.

On the Rota station he made an attack on the night of the 30th Sept., 1811, upon a six-gun battery at Chipiona, and by means of his boats brought out two privateers that had been reposing under its protection. For this he was commended by Rear-Admiral Legge.

In the month of March, 1813, he sailed in the flag-ship *Marlborough* for the Chesapeake.

With his customary daring he led an expedition up the Elk River, which accomplished the expulsion of the enemy from Frenchtown, and the destruction of their dépôts of supplies. Five of the enemy's vessels were burned, and six heavy guns destroyed, altogether involving a loss of more than half a million pounds.

In reference to this exploit, Rear-Admiral Cockburn in his report to the Commander-in-Chief, Sir John Warren, says, " To Lieut. Geo. A Westphal, who has so gallantly conducted and so ably executed this service, my highest encomiums and best acknowledgments are due, and I trust, sir, you will deem him to have merited your favorable consideration and notice."

At Hâvre-de-Grace, on the Susquehanna river, a battery and a large number of houses were destroyed, and the Americans driven to the woods. Lieut. Westphal, who had borne the chief part in this, captured an American officer, took his horse and followed the fugitives alone, altogether forgetting that his followers were on foot. The Americans soon saw this, and turning, they closed round him. Realizing his imminent danger, Westphal rushed at an American officer, and parrying a blow of his sword, caught him up and swung him across his saddle. Though wounded severely, he succeeded in getting safe to camp with his prisoner; his pursuers were close upon him, but his horse was swift of foot. His wound resulted afterwards in the loss of his hand. For this, Rear-Admiral Cockburn reported: "Of Lieut. G. A. Westphal, whose exemplary and gallant conduct it has been necessary for me already to notice in detailing to you the operations of the day, I shall now only add that from a thorough knowledge of his merits, he having served many years with me as first-lieutenant, I always, on similar occasions, expect much from him, but this day he even outstripped these expectations. I therefore, sir, cannot but entertain a confident hope that his services of to-day and the wound he has received, added to what he so succesfully executed at Frenchtown, will obtain for him your favorable consideration and notice, and that of my Lords Commissioners of the Admiralty."

Shortly after this, having gone up the Sassafras river, he assisted in routing four hundred men who had opened fire on the British from an entrenched position, and in demolishing two small towns. In reporting, Admiral Cockburn says of this:— "Lieut Westphal, who had taken his station on the rocket-boat, close to the battery, therefore now judging the moment to be favorable, pulled directly up under the work, and landing with his boat's crew, got immediate possession of it, turned their own guns on them, and thereby obliged them to retreat with their whole force to the farthest extremity of the town, where (the marines having by this time landed) they were closely pursued, and no longer feeling themselves equal to a manly and open resistance, they commenced a teasing and irritating fire from behind the houses, walls and trees, from which I am sorry to say my gallant first-lieutenant received a shot through his hand while leading the pursuing party. He, however, continued to lead the advance with which he soon succeeded in dislodging the whole of the enemy from its lurking-places and driving them from shelter to the neighboring woods; and whilst performing which services he had the satisfaction to overtake, and, with his remaining hand, to take prisoner and bring in an American captain of the militia."

After the attack on Crany Island and the capture of the *Hampton*, he removed with Admiral Cockburn to the *Sceptic* 74. As soon as Portsmouth Island had been captured, Lieut. Westphal, on the 12th May, took command of the advance division of the boats and by pulling straight at the *Anaconda*, he succeeded in capturing her.

Of this vessel, which was taken into the Navy he was made commander. The first duty of importance in his new position was the convoying of twelve valuable vessels from Halifax to the West Indies. During the passage he encountered two American privateers, but after a sharp exchange they were compelled to draw off.

In all the engagements in which he took part, and he was in more than a hundred serious affairs, none was productive of results more important at the juncture than the attack upon New Orleans. The best account of this is in the report of the Commander-in-Chief, Sir A. Cochrane, which is as follows:— "In his endeavours to place the small vessels of war as near as possible to the point of landing, Capt. Westphal was particularly conspicuous in his zeal and success towards the effecting of this important object, he having by the utmost skill, perseverance and exertion, hove the *Anaconda* over a bank nearly five miles in extent, upon which there were only eight feet of water, into Lac Borgne, and occupied a situation that enabled that sloop to render the most essential aid and protection to the open boats conveying troops and supplies from the fleet to the army, which were frequently rescued by her assistance from the imminent danger to which they were reduced by the severity of the weather."

Capt. Westphal, after stationing his vessel, was landed with a division of her seamen, and served in the Naval Brigade, under the command of Sir Thomas Troubridge, who made honourable mention of his exertions.

The *Anaconda* had been stationed in the Gulf, and owing to the prominent situation she had occupied, was fully exposed to the shots of the enemy during the operations of New Orleans. In consequence of the damage received, the *Anaconda* was condemned and sunk.

It is doubtful if any officer in the British service was ever engaged in more persistent and dangerous operations.

He attained the rank of admiral in the year 1819. Subsequently he was employed in conveying the Governor-General of India, and on the occasion of his being knighted in 1824, Sir Robert Peel remarked that "He had been recommended more in consideration of his gallant and distinguished services against the enemy than for his having taken out the Governor-General to India."

He was made Aide-de-Camp to the Queen in 1846.

MAJOR-GENERAL CHARLES BECKWITH, C.B., K.H., K. ST. M. & L.

WAS born at Halifax, Nova Scotia, in October, 1789. He was the eldest son of John Beckwith, Esquire, and Mary, his wife, a sister of the celebrated Judge Haliburton, At fourteen years of age he entered the army. and the esteem in which he was held, as a youth, was an indication of the noble character of his later life. Four years after he had risen to the rank of captain, but so short was he in stature that an old veteran of the 95th regiment used to carry him across deep streams on his back. He sketched himself at this time, with head erect and haughty bearing, in command of soldiers double his own height. But when he had become a major in 1814, he had grown into the stature and appearance befitting an officer.

His active military career began early. In 1807 he went in the expedition against Denmark, and in the following year against Sweden. When Lord Wellesley went to Spain in 1809, Captain Beckwith went under him. Through all the battles of that momentous epoch, Beckwith served. He was at the retreat and battle of Corunna, at Pombal, Fox d'Arona, Salamanca, Orthez, Badajos, Vimiera, Talavera, Ciudad Rodrigo, Toulouse and many others. At Toulouse he received a gold medal which bears this inscription: "Major Charles Beckwith, 95th regiment, Asst. Mr.-Gl., on one side, Victory seated on her car, with a lion at her feet and a laurel crown in her hand: on the other, the simple inscription, 'Toulouse' surrounded by a laural wreath."

Though often in the thickest of the fight, in the many conflicts in which he was engaged at this time, he was not once wounded, but he had many very narrow escapes. As an instance of this, he was one morning, at the outskirts of a wood in which the enemy lay in ambush. His horse was killed under him by a cannon-ball and both rider and horse fell. "I thought for a moment my master was gone," said his faithful old servant; "but just then he rose to his feet exclaiming, 'All right, John,' and by a prompt retreat, placed himself out of reach of the enemy's fire."

At the time of Napoleon's seclusion in Elba, there was a lull in hostilities, and Major Beckwith returned to England where his family had gone from Halifax. "There, as at Halifax, he was the children's best friend, always ready to join in their sports without fear of hurting his dignity." But Napoleon returned from Elba, and the troops of England once more opposed him.

G

At Waterloo Major Beckwith was on Sir James Kempt's staff, and although he had four horses killed under him, he escaped unhurt till the end of the day. As he was riding hurriedly with orders, the last shot fired by the enemy on the field of battle shattered his right leg. He had seen the projectile coming but was unable to get out of the way. In recognition of his services he was raised to the rank of lieut.-colonel and decorated upon the battle-field. He was placed in hospital-quarters, and after a long period of waiting, his leg was amputated.

At this time a remarkable event occurred in his career. The wounded man had been taken to the Château Mont-St. Jean. A little maid of six was his chief and constant nurse. Her childish ways and gentleness moved the heart of the stern soldier. His mind became subdued and reflective. Upon the ground thus prepared fell the seed of religion. His love of glory yielded to the love of God. A copy of the Bible had come into his hands when at Courtray in Belgium. This he now studied very carefully, and as he himself says, "I was carried away by a love of glory, but a good God said to me, 'stop rascal!' and He cut off my leg and now I think I shall be the happier for it."

One of his brother officers who also became a general, thus speaks of him: "I always thought Beckwith the officer in our division who gave the most brilliant hopes for the future, for he possessed all the qualities requisite for the command of an army, great promptitude of conception, imperturbable coolness on the field of battle, an admirable power of organization, and undaunted courage. Although a staff-officer, he was always ready to quit his safe position and throw himself into the thick of the fight, and I remember once seeing him upon the breach at Ciudad-Rodrigo, at the head of the attacking column, though his place ought to have been in the rear of the army. A very remarkable trait in him was the care which he took of the soldiers when he held the post of major-of-brigade. No matter how bad the weather, or how great his own fatigue, he never dismounted until he had seen every one lodged and supplied with every comfort possible in the circumstances. I once heard him advising the soldiers to see that their flannel waist-coats were put on perfectly dry. Whilst not disdaining to attend to such details as these, his fine character, ready wit and cultivated mind made him a favourite at the officers' table and among his companions in arms. I always thought that if he had followed out his career he might have become Commander-in-Chief, for which few were as well qualified as he."

When he had recovered he went back to England to complete his fund of general information and to take a course in theology. From England he returned to pay a visit to the haunts of his childhood in Canada. With the help of a friend, he became the founder of the first Sunday-school of one of the churches of his native place.

To the work of relieving the poor and distressed he devoted a great portion of his time. He travelled widely on this continent for the purpose of extending his knowledge of America. Then he returned to England. In London he was in the habit of meeting with his former comrades of the mess and with his old general, the Duke of Wellington. One day, in 1827, he went to the Duke's residence in Hyde Park. On the table of the library, into which he was shown, lay a book, "Narrative of an excursion to the mountains of Piedmont and researches among the Vaudois or Waldenses, Protestant Inhabitants of the Alps," by Dr. Gilly, of Durham Cathedral. He picked this up and beginning to read became fascinated with the account. So interested had he become in these people that in a very short time he set out for the Vaudois Valleys. The task he had set himself was the evangelization of Italy by means of the Vaudois Church.

He was a man of princely liberality, and attended, with the utmost solicitude, to the care and education of the people.

In a letter of reply to an address of gratitude made to him by the Vaudois students at Berlin and Lausanne, in 1837, is contained a very good review of his work:

SAINT JEAN, 28th June, 1837.

"MY DEAR YOUNG FRIENDS,—It is true that I have for some years been striving to improve public instruction in your country, and that we have succeeded in finding some means which may, in time, be more or less successful. . . . A good education does not consist in variety of information, but in the development of solid qualities of heart and mind.

(Sgd.) CHARLES BECKWITH,

Colonel."

In the following extract from a letter of his to a girl at school, are some characteristic sentiments:

". . . Be true and simple, frank and loving. You have nothing to conceal. Seek the society of the good. . . . When you have once bestowed your confidence and friendship, continue to do so, be slow to give them and slow to withdraw them again. . . The Englishwomen who are now prisoners in Affghanistan have been able to conciliate, by their dignified conduct, the esteem and consideration of the savages around them. It is equally in your power to make the men of this country feel the superiority of your character, of your ideas, your religion, your education and of all that tends to ennoble and elevate the human character."

General Beckwith wrote several works in the Italian language.

A simple but beautiful monument, erected chiefly by the Vaudois, is raised over his grave at Torre-Pellice. On one side is:

TO THE VENERATED MEMORY

OF THEIR ILLUSTRIOUS AND CONSTANT BENEFACTOR,

Major-General Charles Beckwith,

BY THE GRATEFUL VAUDOIS CHURCH.

And on the opposite side:

Born at Halifax, in America, the 2nd October, 1789. *Came for the first time to the Valleys in September,* 1827. *Died at La Tour, the* 19*th July,* 1862.

On the remaining sides are quotations from his own writings.

In 1846 he had become a major-general, and in 1848 he was nominated by King Charles Albert to the rank of Knight of the Order of Saints Maurice and Lazarus.

GENERAL SIR GORDON DRUMMOND, G.C.B.

GORDON DRUMMOND was born at Quebec in 1771. He was the son of Colin Drummond, Esquire, of Megginch, Paymaster-General of the Forces in Lower Canada. He entered the British service as ensign, in the 1st Royal Regiment of Foot. His first appointment was upon the staff of the Earl of Westmoreland, then Lord Lieutenant of Ireland.

He became captain in the 41st Foot, in 1792, then major of the 23rd Foot in 1794, and lieutenant-colonel of the 8th King's Regiment of Foot, the same year.

In command of this regiment he served in Holland under the Duke of York. He received high praise for the good judgment and valour displayed by him during the siege of Nimeguen and at the sortie.

His next station was at Minorca, whither he proceeded with his regiment, and where he remained till the expedition went to Egypt under Sir Ralph Abercrombie. He took part in the battles of the 8th, 13th, and 21st, and in the engagement of Rhamanieh. He was also present at the surrender of Grand Cairo and Alexandria. For his services in this campaign he received a silver medal and clasp. After a short station at Gibraltar, he proceeded, as major-general and second in command to Sir Eyre Coot, to Jamaica. The British authorities had resolved to begin offensive operations against the West Indies, and despatched this expedition for that purpose.

From this position he was removed to the staff in Canada, till 1811, when he received the appointment of the command of the southern district in Ireland.

The government, whilst keeping him nominally in his last command, appointed him lieutenant-general under Sir George Prevost in Canada. He assumed, without delay, control of the troops in Upper Canada, where he prosecuted one of the most vigorous campaigns of the American war.

Fort Niagara was one of the finest strongholds of the Americans, and filled with military stores. To this Lieut.-Gen. Drummond laid siege, and it was taken by storm. His operations against the Americans at Black Rock and at Oswego in company with Commodore Sir James Yeo were well planned and successfully carried out.

At the battle of Lundy's Lane, which was fought chiefly in the darkness, he received a bullet in the neck, but continued upon horseback until his horse was killed under him. In this, the most bloody and im portant battle of that war, he defeated a superior force of Americans under Generals Scott and Browne.

From his place in the field he was called to succeed Sir George Prevost as Commander-in-Chief and Administrator of the Government till 1816, when he returned to England. In 1817 H.R.H. the Prince Regent conferred upon him the Grand Cross of the Bath. In 1825 this distinguished officer became a General of the Army.

He died in London in 1854.

SIR EDWARD WILLIAM CAMPBELL RICH OWEN, K.C.B., G.C.B., G.C.H.

ADMIRAL OF THE BLUE.

THIS naval officer was born in the year 1771, in the Island of Campobello. This island was then in the Province of Nova Scotia, but is now in the Province of New Brunswick. It was granted, originally, by the Lord Governor of Nova Scotia to Sir Edward Owen's father, and is one of the most lovely spots on the continent. The people of the island to the number of several thousand have, almost altogether, assumed the name of "Owen." Sir Edward's brother, Admiral W. Fitzwilliam Owen, a relative of Lady Ritchie, of Ottawa, who, however, was not born there, spent all the latter part of his life on the island, and died there.

Sir Edward's daughter and her family resided on the island till a few years ago, when, minerals having been discovered there, the rights were sold to a company, and she removed to England,

As in the case of others at that time, Edward Owen was entered in the Navy at a very early age, as captain's servant. His first serious step in the service was made when he joined the *Culloden* 74, in 1786. He was transferred shortly afterwards to other vessels, amongst them being the *Leander*, which bore the flag of Commodore Sawyer, at Halifax.

In 1790, having served in the Channel and Mediterranean squadrons, in the *Lowestoffe*, frigate, he passed the examination which gave to him the qualification to command.

He served for three years on the North American, Home, and West Indian stations in the *Thisbe*, to which he had been appointed; in the *Dido*, and the *Vengeance* 74, and in the *Culloden*, under Captain Sir Thomas Rich.

In 1793, he was made lieutenant in the *Fortunée* 36. His next appointment of importance was into the *London* 98, flying the flags of Admirals Rich and Colpoys.

He rose rapidly in the esteem of his superior officers, so that when in Lord Bridport's action he distinguished himself by his brilliant conduct, he was made acting-captain of the *Impregnable* 98, and of the *Charlotte* 100.

In the following year he rejoined Admiral Colpoys in the *London*, and was then put in command of gun-brigs, first in the Thames, and subsequently at the Nore.

In the year 1798, he became post-captain in the *Northumberland* 74, and in 1801, in the *Nemesis*. As captain, he was in command of a squadron off the Scheldt, near Dunkerque, where his skill in reconnoitering and his quickness in evolution gained him honourable mention, and the praise even of the enemy.

As a consequence of these successful manœuvres he received the appointment of senior-officer in the *Immortalité*, and was placed over a large squadron which had been equipped for service during the Peace of Amiens. When the war broke out again he was stationed off the French coast, and he succeeded, in spite of a heavy fire from the batteries on land, in driving ashore and capturing the *Commode* and *Inabordable*.

His patrol was marked by great daring and good fortune, so that the French were kept in a state of continual alarm.

He undertook, in person, the task of reconnoitering, and at the most unexpected times the *Immortalité* appeared under the batteries or threading dangerous shoals. In this way Captain Owen acquired an accurate knowledge of the coast, which was quite invaluable to those engaged in the task of watching the enemy.

The following report to Lord Keith gives a description of these movements.

"In obedience to the orders of Rear-Admiral Montague, and, at 8 o'clock this morning, in company with the *Perseus* and the *Explosion*, bombs commenced an attack on the batteries which protected the town of Dieppe, and vessels building there, in number, seventeen.

"The firing was continued, on both sides, till half-past eleven, when the lee-tide making strong, and the town having taken fire badly in one place and slightly in two others, I caused the bombs to weigh and proceeded with them off St. Valéry-en-Caux, where they are constructing six vessels, and at 3 p.m. opened fire on that place for an hour. The enemy was for the most part driven from their batteries, the inhabitants flying to the country, and judging from the direction in which many of the shells burst, they must have suffered much. . . ."

A powerful division of the great flotilla which the French had formed for the invasion of England was endeavouring to effect a passage from Boulogne to Étaples. This division was attacked by the squadron under the orders of Capt. Owen, and the junction prevented which was to have been one of the links in the chain of Great Britain's destruction.

In his report of July 20, 1804, he says: "The wind set in yesterday strong from the N.E. by N., and made so much sea that the enemy's vessels in the roads of Boulogne became very uneasy, and about 8 p.m., the innermost brigs got under way and worked to windward, whilst some of the luggers ran down apparently for Étaples. Their force was then 45 brigs and 43 luggers. I made signal to look out on these vessels, which was immediately obeyed by the *Harpy*, the *Bloodhound* and the *Archer*, which closed with them, giving their fire to such as attempted to stand off from the land. The *Autumn* was at this time getting under way, and lost no time in giving her support to the vessels already on this service, and continued with them during the weathertide, firing from time to time on such of the enemy's vessels as gave them opportunity. At daylight this morning there were 19 frigates and 18 luggers only remaining in the bay, and about six o'clock these began to slip single and run to the southward for Étaples."

The remaining British ships now stood in for Boulogne. The wind had increased again and completed the destruction of the Frenchmen. In reference to some of the captains and other officers under him, Commodore Owen, as he was now, observes: " There cannot be any doubt but that their well-timed attack caused the enemy's confusion and occasioned much of the loss." The total loss was very great. In addition to the wreck of ships and the destruction of their crews, hundreds of soldiers were killed.

According to the French account, Napoleon was an eye-witness of it all, and was much moved with chagrin and disappointment. He had made Boulogne the chief point of preparation for his grand armament.

In command of a division of six men-o'-war, Owen cruised off this place.

Napoleon, in person, had gone through a minute inspection of the outfittings and had given to them the stamp of his approval. As soon as the gun-brigs got under way, Owen attacked them. These at first resisted, but being joined by others to the number of fifty brigs and many luggers, they weighed anchor again, this time being under command of Napoleon himself, attended by his admirals and generals. But Captain Owen, nothing daunted, boldly attacked them again, and in spite of the fact that the enemy's brigs kept well within range of their own batteries, his squadron stood in to give battle.

So successfully was the attack managed that, notwithstanding the disparity in strength, great damage was done to the French vessels, many of which were compelled to run ashore to save the lives of their men.

By this time the fire of the batteries became too hot, and the squadron retired to resume patrol.

Not long after, the marine sentinels caught sight of another large portion of the flotilla with the usual complement of brigs and luggers, having on board a large contingent of horse-artillery. These were proceeding under guard of the land-batteries. On this occasion, more than on any other, Captain Owen's accurate knowledge of the coast was of great service. Though the French vessels kept perilously near the shore, the British squadron maintained a running fire, much to the enemy's injury and annoyance.

On the 18th of July, 1805, Captain Owen had gone to windward off Cape Gregory to watch the way to the rendezvous at Boulogne. In shore the shoals were most dangerous, but notwithstanding this, the British ships, handled with the energy and spirit which the importance of the occasion demanded, attacked another and very large squadron, almost wholly destroying it. Many ships that were not sunk in battle ran on shore and were wrecked.

From this station Captain Owen was called home to guard the embarkation of troops. However, this lasted but a short time, and in October, 1806, the first experimental trial of the famous Congreve rockets was entrusted to him. He proceeded to Boulogne and under cover of darkness wrought immense damage to the town and to the vessels in the harbour.

In 1809, as commodore, he was appointed to accompany the Walcheren Expedition, that most unfortunate interference of England in the Franco-Austrian troubles.

In this he greatly distinguished himself, receiving the highest praise for his placing of the guns in the attack on Flushing. The batteries having been completed, and the frigates, bombs and gun-vessels having at the same time taken their stations under Capts Cockburn and Owen, a fire was opened at half-past one in the day from fifty pieces of heavy ordnance, which was vigorously replied to by the enemy. An additional battery of six guns was made, and the whole continued the bombardment. Sir Richard Strachan says of him, in his report of August 17. . . . "Capt. Owen, of the *Clyde*, with equal skill and judgment, placed the bombs and other vessels under his orders."

As a skilful handler of heavy guns he had earned a high reputation. At one time the *Blake*, the flagship of Rear-Admiral Lord Gardner, was in the utmost peril. She had run aground in the very teeth of the batteries immediately after the grounding of the Admiral's flagship, the *San Domingo*. The battery opened fire, but by the exceptional adroitness of the gunners

H

under Capt. Owen, it was kept in check until the ships were got off.

"In addition," Admiral Strachan continues, "to my despatch this morning, I have now to transmit a letter and an extract of one I have just received from Commodore Owen. Every time I hear from that gallant officer I have just cause to admire his conduct."

On the 13th of February, 1813, he was appointed to the *Cornwall* 74, stationed in the North Sea, off Texel, and in December he distinguished himself by his exemplary conduct at the head of the Royal Marines, landed from the British fleet to co-operate with the Dutch royalists in expelling the French from South Beveland.

For a brief period after this, Commander Owen was in command of the Royal Yacht. From this he went upon the West Indies station.

During his period of service there, in the troubles peculiar to those islands, he received the thanks of the Jamaica Assembly. In 1815, he was nominated a K.C.B., and in the year 1821 he received the appointment of Colonel of the Royal Marines. In the *Gloucester* 74, he cruised as commodore until 1825, when he attained flag-rank.

In 1828 he held the general command in the East Indies station. As Sir E. W. R. C. Owen he sat in parliament, in 1826, for Sandwich, and in the following year was appointed to the high position of Surveyor-General of the Ordnance.

The distinguished honour of membership of the Council of the Lord High Admiral was then conferred upon him, and in 1832 he was nominated a G.C.H. The last decoration bestowed upon him before retirement was that of the Grand Cross of the Bath in 1845.

SIR EDWARD BELCHER, KT., C. B., F. R. A. S., F.G.S.

VICE-ADMIRAL.

EDWARD BELCHER was born in Halifax, Nova Scotia, in the year 1799. He was the second son of the Hon. Andrew Belcher, a member of the Legislative Council of Nova Scotia, grandson of Jonathan Belcher, Chief Justice, and afterwards Governor of Halifax, and great-grandson of James Belcher, who had been Governor of Massachusetts, New Hampshire and New Jersey, and who was so intimately connected with New England history. His mother was Miss von Gear, an American lady. He received his education at the college at Halifax.

As a first-class volunteer he entered H. M. Navy in April, 1812, on board the *Abercrombie* 74.

In the same year he attained the rating of midshipman. Shortly after this he was removed into the *Bellerophon* 74, flag-ship at Newfoundland of Sir Richard Goodwin Keats. After cruising for some time he was appointed to the *Malta* 84, and fought in her at the defence of Gaëta.

As the barbarian rulers of Algiers at this time had enslaved the Christians and were issuing mandates for their further ill-treatment, England decided to interfere. A large fleet was sent out under Lord Exmouth. The *Superb*, to which Belcher had been appointed, was one of this squadron. On the 27th day of August, 1816, was fought the battle of Algiers, a most sanguinary and bitter conflict. Victory finally remained with the British, and the Christians were released. For his courage and address in this battle, Captain Elkins " recommended " him to the notice of his chief.

From the *Superb* he was removed to the *Sybill*, a flag-ship at Jamaica of Sir Home Pophan. He was then sent to the African station in the *Myrmidon*, having received his first commission in the year 1818. Owing to the unhealthiness of the African climate, he was obliged to place himself on the "Invalid List" for one year. However, having restored his health, he remained in the Halifax station for two years, in the *Salisbury* 50. In all his various stations he had attracted the attention of his superior officers by his scientific attainments.

When the expedition under Captain Beechy was fitted out for a voyage to the Behring Strait, *via* Cape Horn, to seek a north-west passage, Lieut. Belcher was chosen as Captain Beechy's assistant in the *Blossom*. From a scientific point of view the expedition was most successful. The *Blossom* co-operated with other expeditions by land, and the result so much desired was gained. In her voyage through the Pacific, Captain Beechy took possession of several groups of islands, and strategic stations in many places have been established upon them. At length, after a voyage of seventy-three thousand miles, sailed during an absence of three years and a half, the *Blossom* returned to England, having rendered most signal services to the science of navigation, as well as in less important ways.

For his share in this voyage, and in appreciation of the admirable maps he had made of many safe harbours for British vessels, he was immediately raised to the position of commander. This appointment was made while he was on board the *Southampton*, flagship of Admiral E. W. R. C. Owen.

Commander Belcher was then despatched to explore the coast of Africa. Having succeeded in acquiring the necessary information, he was sent to Spain to protect British interests during the misunderstanding between Spain and Portugal, and from this he joined the Mediterranean fleet. In 1841 he came into prominence as a naval officer of some note.

It will be remembered that in the war between Great Britain and China, a system of tactics was adopted by the British, suitable to the peculiar character of their antagonists. Much depended on the steadiness and resource of those actually engaged in carrying out the orders of their superior officers. Early in the year 1841, Commander Belcher, who had succeeded to the command of H.M.S. *Sulphur*, was directed by Captain Herbert, the senior officer in the division of the squadron in which he was, to attack and sink, if possible, a large fleet of war-junks. From the shallowness of the water it was possible to employ only the *Nemesis* and ship's boats

At the first moment of action the *Nemesis* succeeded in blowing up the Chinese admiral's flag-ship, and so hot was their fire that the Chinese fled precipitately. Commander Belcher was highly praised for his conduct of this affair, as the style of attack was in the nature of an experiment, and he " showed to every advantage the powerful force of this description of war-steamer, combining as she does a commanding armament with a light draught."

In March following, the enemy had formally established themselves at Junk Reach. Sir J. J. Gordon Bremer, the commodore in command, decided to attack them. In his report he says:—" On the following morning I detached that ever-ready officer, Commander Belcher, in the *Sulphur*, up Junk River to reconnoitre, that ship being taken in tow .... the position seemed formidable, and on the 5th of May the Major-General and myself prepared to attack it. ... On the approach of the *Sulphur*, which led, the enemy opened fire, but were in a short time silenced and compelled to flee." This exploit removed the defences of Canton between that place and the sea, and was followed up by a concerted attack on the Chinese forts of Chuenpee and Tycocktow.

The conduct of the attack upon the upper fort was entrusted to Commander Belcher, who moved the *Sulphur* into position, and directing the *Queen* and *Nemesis* to take their stations close at hand, he proceeded to shell the fortress. In a few hours he had destroyed a great part of it and inflicted serious loss upon the enemy A little to the eastward of this position eleven Chinese war-junks were anchored.

Accompanied by the *Starling* and the boats of the *Calliope*, by an adroit movement he got in amongst them and completely destroyed them. Shortly after this he made the following report to Capt. Senlouse:—

"Off Canton in H.M.S. *Sulphur*.

"In pursuance of your directions I proceeded up the creek on the western side of Canton, in order to examine the nature of the country, our force consisting of the *Druid's* launch, gigs, cutters, &c. On approaching Neshang where the boats of the squadron were yesterday engaged, I observed the "fast boats" of the enemy collected in great numbers. I retreated up the creek to the left, but shortly after returned and drew up. An attack was made and many of the Chinese boats destroyed." Proceeding, he says, "The enemy being posted on the hill above us, prevented me, in obedience to your orders, from exposing my small party by an attempt to dislodge them, but I fully succeeded in effecting my reconnoitre by being hoisted to the mast-head of the largest junk, from whence I was able to survey the whole country.

"(Signed.) ED. BELCHER,
Commander."

The next movement of decisive importance was the attack on Canton, in October, 1841, This city contained a million and a half inhabitants, and was strongly fortified. The attacking force amounted to three thousand five hundred men. It was necessary that soundings should be obtained in order that Sir Hugh Gough might be enabled to land his forces. These were undertaken and successfully made by Commander Belcher, who was exposed to the continual fire of the enemy. But amongst the most stirring incidents that occurred during the siege of this place was the destruction of a masked battery by Commander Belcher. This battery was of great strength, and he was "distinguished for his great bravery." The capture of Canton virtually ended the war, and Commander Belcher was left to the more profitable employment of surveying in the East Indies and along the coast of South America.

In consideration of his services in this war he was raised to the rank of post-captain in 1841, and was made a Companion of the Bath. He was further made a K.C.B. in 1843, and in 1847 he retired from active service and was paid off. In due course he was raised to the rank of Vice-Admiral.

He had been entrusted with one of the numerous expeditions in search of Capt. McClure and Sir John Franklin, but returned unsuccessful after having endured great hardships.

During his long voyages, in the course of his extensive explorations, whilst in command of the *Sulphur*, he acquired much valuable information which he published under the title of "A Narrative of a Voyage Round the World in H. M. S. *Sulphur*." This is considered an important work. He wrote also a "Treatise on Nautical Surveying," which was thought one of the ablest upon the subject at that time.

He died a few years ago in England.

LIEUT-GENERAL SIR RICHARD ENGLAND, G.C.B., K.H.

RICHARD ENGLAND was born at Detroit towards the close of the last century,
At this time Detroit was a part of Canada. He entered the Army as ensign in the 50th Regiment of Foot or Queen's Own, becoming lieutenant the following year. His first experience of moment was in the disastrous Walcheren Expedition, where delay and sickness played such havoc with the British forces.

In August, 1809, the English army had succeeded in closely investing the fortress of Flushing, which had been admirably prepared to withstand a siege. Owing to the inability of the commander of the expeditionary force to cut off all the avenues to Flushing, the garrison had been greatly increased by accessions of troops until it amounted to ten thousand men. The besieged made many daring sorties, but in no case were they successful.

It was then the intention of the military authorities to blockade this place by the co-operation of the fleet with the army, but, owing to the peculiarly stormy weather that prevailed, this was not accomplished for some time. When the junction was made, however, and the stronghold vigorously attacked, it was speedily reduced, and its capitulation followed on the 13th of August.

The 50th Regiment was in Major-General Dyot's brigade, and was highly praised by that officer as well as by Sir Eyre Coot.

It was part of the French policy at this time to acquire the island of Sicily. King Murat threatened it with invasion, and its inhabitants were inclined to submit. This the English viewed with alarm, and General Stewart was despatched with a small force for the purpose of arousing the Sicilians to a sense of their duty.

About the middle of October, taking advantage of the favourable winds, King Murat landed a body of troops. The English and Sicilians combined under General Stewart and resisted this attack successfully. In the battle which followed, the 50th, in which England was lieutenant, did valiant service. It was to no purpose, however, as the islanders became indifferent and were induced away from British influence.

At this time England received his commission as captain in that regiment.

The war with Napoleon, in Spain, had begun, and Captain England entered it, taking part in many battles of that stirring period, and receiving, as a mark of honour for his services, the right to have the letter ℞ prefixed to his official title.

He was also with the army in Paris in 1815. In 1825, he was raised to the rank of lieutenant-colonel and appointed to the 41st Regiment. From this he was transferred to the 75th, which he commanded for several years.

In 1834-35, there had been a serious irruption of the Kaffirs into Cape Colony, with the result that many lives were lost and much property destroyed. Emboldened by the fact that no revenge had been taken for these raids, in 1836-37, began what is known as the Kaffir War. England was sent out by the government as Commandant of Kaffraria, and under him the conflict was ended and order restored.

For these services he received a medal and was advanced to a full colonelcy.

In 1842, was brought to an inglorious close one of the most appalling failures that the British Army has ever met with. Actuated by an ambition to gain renown in extending the north-western boundary of India, the Governor-General of that dependency ordered a general advance into Affghanistan. Under the pretence of deposing one prince to enthrone another, the British forces marched into that country, but the army had not been increased to a war-footing, and, besides, several large rivers separated the base of supplies from the main body of men.

Affghanistan was divided into five districts, of which the cities of Herat, Khelat, Cabool, Peshawur, and Kandahar were the important centres. The country, extremely mountainous, affords many defences for a brave, warlike and independent people such as the Affghans are. The invasion resulted in the disasters of Jellalabad and Ghuznee.

Realizing the mistake made, the Governor decided to withdraw, at the earliest moment, from the campaign, and the retreat to the Indus began.

At this time Brigadier England was in command of the Sindh field-force at Dadni, where he received instructions to penetrate at once the Bolan Pass, and to march to Quettah. At this place he was to be reenforced. The additional troops did not come, however, and alarmed at the probable condition of the retreating column, as well as by the note of his instructions, which were to push on to Kojuck, Brigadier England, on the 22nd of March, set out, drawing up finally in the Pisheen Valley.

General Nott was to have joined him with several

regiments, but as he failed in this, Brigadier England's position became an unenviable one.

He has been blamed for over-rashness in leaving Quettah without reinforcements, but it must be remembered that in addition to his instructions he was promised that several regiments should meet him on the march. So desperate was the situation that officers in England's brigade openly prophesied that they would never reach Kojuck Pass alive, and the state of affairs was not rendered more reassuring by their entire unacquaintance with the country and their ignorance of the whereabouts of the enemy.

Moreover, English agents sent out with information were themselves misinformed.

In the course of the march the brigade came suddenly upon the enemy behind the heights of Hykulzye, under Mahmoud Sadig. After a consultation, an attack was made and a desperate contest ensued. The Affghans were not driven from their position, but they received a severe check. As they became reinforced, Brigadier England deemed it wise to retreat with his small body of men.

Because some of his officers wished to rush upon the enemy once more, he has been found fault with for not ordering another attack. Had he done so and failed, not a man would have escaped, and all the supplies and treasure of which they were the custodians would have fallen into the enemy's hands.

After having withdrawn and ascertained thoroughly the nature of the country, he ordered an advance upon Hykulzye again. The Affghans, confident of success, were on the heights as before, but the troops were in a state of exasperation and they drove them back in confusion. The infantry, following on, completed their rout.

On the 30th of April, England's brigade entered Kojuck Pass. Here he was joined by General Nott. They marched to Kandahar, the prisoners were rescued, and the retreat to India was brought to a successful conclusion.

The end of this doubtful campaign was proclaimed in Lord Ellenborough's celebrated "Manifesto of the Gates."

For his services in this campaign, Brigadier England was decorated and promoted.

His next appearance was in the Russian war.

When the allied armies entered the Crimea, Major-General England was chosen to command the third division of the British force.

At the battle of the Alma he supported the first division in the attack upon the centre and right of the enemy. The operations were successful, and he was very cordially thanked by Lord Raglan.

At another time, on the 5th of November, when the Russians made the most determined of their sorties, his division played a most important part in their repulse.

" I must likewise express my obligations to Lieutenant-General England for the excellent disposition he made of his division and the assistance he rendered to the left. (Sgd.) RAGLAN."

He had received his appointment as lieutenant-general on the fourth of June. For his valuable services in that war, and particularly for his skill in commanding on the south side of Sebastopol throughout the investment, he received a medal, with clasps for Alma, Inkerman and Sebastopol, the orders of the Grand Cross of the Bath and the K.H.

* Decorations.

1. Medal for Peninsular War.
2. Medal for Kaffir War.
3. Medal for Affghan War.
4. Medal and clasps for the Crimean War.
5. Orders of G.C.B., K.H.
6. First class of the Medjidie.
7. Grand Officer of the Legion of Honour and Sardinian medal.

LIEUT.-GENERAL DANIEL BABY

DANIEL BABY was the son of the Hon. Jacques Duperron Baby and Susanne de la Croix Réaume. He was born at Detroit, then in Canadian territory, where his father had gone to repair his fortunes that had been ruined by the war.

Daniel Baby entered the service at an early age as lieutenant in H.M. 24th Regiment of Foot. He served throughout the Peninsular war under the Duke of Wellington. *Il acheva de se couvrir de gloire au siége de Badajos**. At this siege two of his compatriots of the de Salaberry family were killed, but Lieutenant Baby came safely through. He then served in India for many years, rising to the rank of lieutenant-general. He died in London in 1861, leaving an only son, born in England, however, who entered the Army.

---

* *Histoire des grandes familles françaises.* The fortress of Badajos was the work of General Vicompte DeLéry, a French-Canadian in Napoleon's army, who, as chief engineer of the French, planned the fortifications of the Rhine, etc. He was one of the greatest of military engineers.

MAJOR-GENERAL EDWARD ANDREW STUART.

LIEUTENANT-GOVERNOR OF THE ROYAL HOSPITAL, CHELSEA.

EDWARD ANDREW STUART was born in the city of Quebec, and is a son of the late Chief Justice Sir James Stuart, Bart., of that place. His family has been prominent for a long period in the affairs of Lower Canada.

He entered the army in the 1st Royal Regiment of Foot, as ensign, serving through the Crimean war. At Inkerman he received a very severe wound which incapacitated him for some time. He served, also, throughout the war in China of 1860, and was at the taking of Sinho and Tangku, the occupation of Tientsin and the surrender of Pekin.

An outrage had been perpetrated upon the British flag on board the *Lorcha Arrow*, in 1857, at Canton. The insult was not as speedily atoned for as it might have been, and England declared war. Fearful of the consequences, the Chinese sued for peace and a compromise was effected. Sir Frederick Bruce, when on his way to Pekin, in fulfilment of this compromise, in 1860, accompanied by a naval escort, was fired upon.

Immediately the English and French governments despatched a force under Sir Hope Grant to move on Pekin. Though the commander of the allied troops gained some successes at first, his force was surprised and many prisoners were taken and conveyed to Pekin.

In the end, however, the Chinese were beaten and those prisoners who outlived their tortures were restored to the allies.

For this breach of faith, severe punishment was inflicted upon the enemy, and the campaign was brought to a close.

Colonel Stuart's last appointment was upon the staff of the Royal Hospital, Chelsea.

"ROYAL HOSPITAL, Chelsea.

"Lieutenant-Colonel and Colonel E. A. Stuart, now commanding the 1st Regimental District (the Royal Scots, Lothian Regiment), to be Major and Lieutenant-Governor, *vice* Colonel R. Wadeson, V.C., deceased."

He has been advanced recently to the rank of a general officer, and is the second representative of the 1st Foot of that rank on the active list.

Decorations.

1. Crimean medal and clasps.
2. The Medjidie of the fifth class.
3. The Turkish medal.
4. The Chinese medal and two clasps.

The Victoria Cross.

V.C. COLONEL ALEXANDER ROBERTS DUNN

ALEXANDER ROBERTS DUNN was born in the city of Toronto, and was the second son of the Honourable John H. Dunn, for twenty years the Receiver-General of Canada. His mother was a member of the Duchesnay family, of Quebec.

At an early age he exhibited a strong inclination for military life. He was a handsome man of a rather mild cast of features, but possessed of singularly great personal strength and daring, so that he was well equipped for that arduous calling.

On the 11th of March, 1852, he became a cornet in the 11th Hussars. In the following year he was raised to the rank of lieutenant and, as such, entered the Crimean war, serving in the battles of Inkermann and Alma and at Sebastopol. At Balaklava he won the Cross of Valour. In the celebrated charge of the Six Hundred, when Lord Cardigan, clad in the brilliant uniform of the 11th Hussars, led the Light Brigade, the 11th were on the extreme left of the column. When they had charged through the Russian battery they drew up to reform, for coming straight at them was a body of Russian cavalry, of overwhelming numbers. But at this moment a most peculiar circumstance intervened. The Russian colonel made sure that no *small* body of men could have done what they had, and, without more, he came forward and surrendered his sword to Lieut. Palmer.

Of all that corps but fifty now remained. Yet again the 11th charged, and the Russian reinforcements that had come up in large numbers turned at the mad onset and fled. But miracles could no longer be performed. The main body of the enemy had arrived, and the 11th being overpowered, were compelled to retreat. Joining the few that were left of the 4th Hussars, they cut their way back. Dunn's horse had been shot under him, but he sprang upon one that was rushing riderless about the field, and it was then that, seeing Sergt. Bentley beset by three Russian lancers, who were in the act of killing him, he, without a moment's hesitation, attacked them, and by the strength of his arm and the vigour of his charge, succeeded in cutting down the three.

A little further on the Russians had flocked together and attacked, in small bands, individual members of the 11th.

A Russian hussar, with others, had fallen upon Private Levett, and was about to cut him down when

Lieut. Dunn, bursting through, rushed upon the officer and with an avenging sweep, slew him.

For these daring deeds he was recommended, with one accord, by his companions-in-arms, for the Victoria Cross when Her Majesty instituted that token of honour.

This badge of "conspicuous bravery" carries with it the stamp of individual valour as no other symbol has ever done. Courage is the one passport to its possession. It is awarded with the utmost caution, and the humblest soldier has the same chance of winning it as his officer.

"It bears upon it the very image and superscription, as it were, of each valiant man upon whom it may be conferred." Medals are usually given for courage and steadiness in battle where numbers take part in the attack or defence. In this case it is for *individual* heroism. This order is held in higher respect amongst military men than any other.

As the origin and history of it is not generally understood, a short account is given below :—

ROYAL WARRANT INSTITUTING VICTORIA CROSS.

Extract from London Gazette, Feb. 5, 1856.

War Department, Feb. 5, 1856.

The Queen has been pleased, by an instrument under Her Royal Sign Manual, of which the following is a copy, to institute and create a new naval and military decoration, to be styled and designated "The Victoria Cross," and to make the rules and regulations therein set forth under which the said decoration shall be conferred.

> *Victoria*, by the Grace of God of the United Kingdom of Great Britain and Ireland, Queen, Defender of the Faith, &c.
>
> To all to whom those presents shall come, greeting.—

Whereas We, taking into Our Royal consideration that there exists no means of adequately rewarding the individual gallant services, either of officers of the lower grades in our naval and military service, or of warrant and petty officers, seamen and marines in our Navy, and non-commissioned officers and soldiers in our Army; and, whereas, the Third Class of our most Honourable Order of the Bath is limited, except in very rare cases, to the higher ranks of both services, and the granting of medals, both in our Navy and Army, is only awarded for long service or meritorious conduct, rather than for bravery in action or distinction before an enemy, such cases alone excepted where a general medal is granted for a particular action or campaign, or a clasp added to the medal for some special engagement, in both of which cases all share equally in the boon, and those who, by their valour, have particularly signalised themselves remain undistinguished from their comrades: Now, for the purpose of attaining an end so desirable as that of rewarding individnal instances of merit and valour, we have instituted and created, and by these presents for Us, Our Heirs and Successors, institute and create a new naval and military decoration, which We are desirous should be highly prized and eagerly sought after by the officers and men of our naval and military services, and are graciously pleased to make, ordain and establish the following rules and ordinances for the government of the same, which shall from henceforth be inviolably observed and kept.

Firstly. It is ordained that the distinction shall be styled and designated "The Victoria Cross," and shall consist of a Maltese Cross of bronze, with Our Royal Crest in the centre, and underneath with an escroll bearing this inscription : " For Valour."

Secondly. It is ordained that the cross shall be suspended from the left breast, by a blue riband for the Navy and by a red riband for the Army.

Thirdly. It is ordained that the names of those upon whom We may be pleased to confer the decorations, shall be published in the London *Gazette*, and a registry thereof kept in the office of Our Secretary of State for War.

Fourthly. It is ordained that any one who, after having received the cross, shall again perform an act of bravery, which, if he had not received such cross would have entitled him to it, such further act shall be recorded by a bar attached to the riband by which the cross is suspended, and for every additional act of bravery an additional bar may be added.

Fifthly. It is ordained that the cross shall only be awarded to those officers or men who have served us in the presence of the enemy, and shall have then performed some signal act of valour or devotion to their country.

Sixthly. It is ordained with a view to place all persons on a perfectly equal footing in relation to eligibility for the decoration, that neither rank, nor long service, nor wounds, nor any other circumstance or condition whatsoever, save the merit of conspicuous bravery, shall be held to establish a sufficient claim to the honour.

Seventhly. It is ordained that the decoration may be conferred on the spot where the act to be rewarded by the grant of such decoration has been performed, under the following circumstances :

1. When the fleet or army, in which such act has been performed, is under the eye and command of an admiral or general officer commanding the forces.

2. When the naval or military force is under the eye or command of an admiral or commodore commanding a squadron or detached naval force, or of a general commanding a corps, or division, or brigade, on a distinct and detached service, when such admiral, commodore or general officer shall have the power of conferring the decoration on the spot, subject to confirmation by Us.

Eighthly. It is ordained, where such act shall not have been performed in sight of a commanding officer as aforesaid, then the claimant for the honour shall prove the act to the satisfaction of the captain or officer commanding his ship, or to the officer commanding the regiment to which the claimant belongs, and such captain or such commanding officer shall report the same through the usual channel to the admiral or commodore commanding the force employed on the service, or to the officer commanding the forces on the field, who shall call for such description or attention of the admiral as he may think requisite, and on approval shall recommend the grant of the decoration.

Ninthly. It is ordained that every person selected for the cross, under rule seven, shall be publicly decorated before the naval or military force or body to which he belongs and with which the act of bravery for which he is to be rewarded shall have been performed, and his name shall be recorded in a general order, together with the cause of his especial distinction.

Tenthly. It is ordained that every person selected under rule eight shall receive his decoration as soon as possible, and his name shall likewise appear in a general order as above required, such general order to be opened by the naval or military commander of the force employed on the service.

Eleventhly. It is ordained that the general order above referred to shall from time to time be transmitted to our Secretary of State for War, to be laid before us and shall be by him registered.

Twelfthly. It is ordained that as cases may arise not falling within the rules above specified, or in which a claim, though well founded, may not have been established on the spot, we will, on the joint submission of our own Secretary of State for War, and of our Commander-in-Chief of our army, or on that of our Lord High Admiral or Lord Commissioner of the Admiralty in the case of the navy, confer the decoration, but never without conclusive proof of the performance of the act of bravery for which the claim is made.

Thirteenthly. It is ordained that, in the event of a gallant and daring act having been performed by a squadron, ship's company, a detached body of seamen and marines, not under fifty in number, or by a brigade, regiment, troop, or company in which the admiral, general, or other officer commanding such forces may deem that all are equally brave and distinguished and that no special selection can be made by them; then in such case the admiral, general, or other officer commanding, may direct that for any such body of seamen or marines, or for every troop or company of soldiers, one officer shall be selected by the officers engaged for this decoration, and in like manner one petty officer, or non-commissioned officer, shall be selected by the petty officers and non-commissioned officers engaged; and two seamen, or private soldiers, or marines, shall be selected by the seamen or private soldiers or marines engaged respectively, for decoration, and the names of those selected shall be transmitted by the senior officer in command of the naval, force, brigade, regiment, troop, or company, to the admiral or general officer commanding, who shall in due manner confer the decoration as if the acts were done under his own eye.

Fourteenthly. It is ordained that every warrant officer, petty officer, seaman, or marine, or non-commissioned officer, or soldier, who shall have received the cross shall from the date of the act by which the decoration has been gained, be entitled to a special pension of ten pounds a year, and each additional bar conferred under rule four on such warrant, or petty officer, or non-commissioned officer, or marine, shall carry with it an additional pension of five pounds per annum.

Fifteenthly, In order to make such additional provisions as shall effectually preserve pure this most honourable distinction, it is ordained that if any person on whom such distinction shall be conferred be convicted of treason, cowardice, felony, or of an infamous crime, or if he be accused of any such offence and doth not after a reasonable time surrender himself to be tried for the same, his name shall be forthwith erased from the registry of indivduals upon whom the said decoration shall have been conferred, by an especial warrant under our Royal Sign Manual, and the pension conferred under rule fourteen shall cease and determine from the date of such warrant. It is hereby further declared that We, Our heirs and successors, shall be the sole judges of the circumstances demanding such expulsion, moreover we shall at all times have power to restore such persons as may at any time have been expelled both to the enjoyment of the decoration and pension.

    Given at Our Court, at Buckingham Palace, this twenty-ninth day of January, in the nineteenth year of Our reign, and in the year of Our Lord, one thousand eight hundred and fifty-six.

        By Her Majesty's command.

        (Signed.)   PANMURE.

To Our Principal Secretary
   of State for War.

The inauguration of this order of valour was held on June 26th, 1857. Nothing was left undone to add to the splendour and importance of the occasion. The weather was all that could have been wished, and Hyde Park never looked gayer than on that day.

At nine o'clock, the advance-guard came upon the ground and was formed into line. This was followed by the artillery and cavalry, who then took up their positions. Those who were to receive the Victoria Cross stood in single file facing the troops, officers and privates—grenadiers, hussars, artillerymen and sailors—stood together, without distinction, and when they drew up the cheers of tens of thousands greeted them. At ten minutes to ten o'clock a flash from the right and a heavy boom announced the approach of the Royal procession. First came the generals and aides-de-camp, to the number of fifty, gleaming in the stars of their several orders and in the lustre of all their decorations.

Next in order rode His Royal Highness, the General Commander-in-Chief, then Her Majesty, the Queen, upon a cream-coloured steed, with Prince Albert upon the right and Prince William, of Prussia, upon the left, followed by the Royal Family in carriages.

It is needless to say that the vast crowd cheered their welcome to the echo. It was a most splendid spectacle—the gathering of the chivalry of the British Empire upon this occasion. Valour has at all times won the world's applause, and the reward of valour has always moved men's admiration. It was indeed a thrilling sight—these fifty men, chosen out of all the brave of the British Navy and the British Army, bearing the marks of dangers faced and perils overcome—" the bravest of the brave,"—and the men felt the solemnity of the event, for now, for all time, was to be founded this " Order of Heroes."

Upon the arrival of the Queen, the ceremony began. One by one the names were called, the men stepped forward, and as each approached, Her Majesty received the decoration from Lord Panmure, and bending from the saddle fixed it upon the breast of the recipient, who then retired to the line in the rear.

The men of the Navy came first, the Royal Marines next, and then the members of the Army, of whom Lieut. Dunn was the third in number.

When the last decoration had been bestowed the six thousand troops were put through a few movements, and the Royal cortége, having re-formed, departed midst the deafening cheers of the great concourse.

Nearly every regiment had a pet animal with it. The Guards had a noble-looking Newfoundland dog, and a large shaggy one of the same species accompanied another regiment.

" This dog, on arriving at a point in front of Her Majesty, seated himself with a look of profound complacency and so remained until the last rank of his regiment had passed. He then rose and took his place between the two officers, and brought up the rear."

The cross is not a gaudy jewel, but is made simply and of gun-metal, in the Maltese pattern. The design is the Lion and the Crown, and below the expressive words, "For Valour." It is pendant from a blue riband for the Navy and a red one for the Army. Each member of the order has written before his name the letters "V.C."

On this occasion it was made from the cannon captured from the Russians. From the date of the act which gives this decoration all non-commissioned officers and privates are entitled to a pension of £10 a year, and for each bar won thereafter £5 a year additional.

It is not probable that the Sovereign will ever again bestow the decorations in person, for, by the Royal Warrant, the commander-in-chief is empowered to give the cross upon the field of battle.

The period of activity enjoyed by the 11th Hussars in the Crimea was succeeded by a home station, which lasted nearly ten years. Lieut. Dunn retired by the sale of his commission on the 12th of January, 1855, and returned to Canada.

When the 100th was formed in 1858 he exerted himself strongly in raising the regiment, and as he was a soldier of approved daring and experience, the rank of "Major" was conferred upon him.

In June, 1861, his appointment as lieut.-colonel was gazetted.

Not long after he retired from the 100th, which was doing merely garrison-duty, and on the 20th of December, 1864, he was appointed Lieutenant-Colonel of the 33rd, or Duke of Wellington's Regiment of Foot, which had won its laurels at Seringapatam, Waterloo, and in the Crimea.

This regiment went to India, too late, however, to take part in the suppression of the Indian mutiny, but its thirst for glory was appeased by the honour conferred upon it in the Abyssinian war. To the men of the 33rd was assigned the task of making the first attack on the Magdala. The fighting was more stubborn than was expected, but after a hard struggle they captured the citadel and burst in the gate, only to find that King Theodore, clad in simple garb, lay dead, killed by his own hand.

Whilst out hunting in Abyssinia, Colonel Dunn was slain, in what way or by whom is still a mystery.

Decorations.

1. Crimean War medal with four clasps.
2. The Turkish medal.
3. The Victoria Cross.

V.C. HERBERT TAYLOR READE, C.B.,
SURGEON-GENERAL.

HERBERT TAYLOR READE was born at Perth, in the Province of Ontario, on Sept. 20th, 1828, and is the son of the late Staff-Surgeon G. H. Reade, formerly lieutenant-colonel commanding the 3rd Regiment of Canadian Militia.

On the 8th November, 1850, he was gazetted to H. M. 61st Regiment, and served in it throughout the Indian Mutiny. He was in the attack on Ferozopore, the siege, assault and capture of Delhi, and the assault on the Magazine. For these services he was mentioned in the despatches and received the Victoria Cross. The act of bravery for which this decoration was awarded is described as follows in the *London Gazette*: "During the siege of Delhi, on the 14th Sept., 1857, while Surgeon Reade was attending to the wounded, at the end of one of the streets of the city, a party of rebels advanced from the direction of the bank, and having established themselves in the houses in the street, commenced firing from the roof. The wounded were thus in very great danger and would have fallen into the hands of the enemy had not Surgeon Reade drawn his sword and calling upon the few soldiers who were near to follow, succeeded under a heavy fire in dislodging the rebels from their position.

"Surgeon Reade's party consisted of about ten in all of whom two were killed and five or six wounded.

"Surgeon Reade also accompanied the regiment at the assault of Delhi, and on the morning of the 16th September, 1857, was one of the first up at the breach of the Magazine, which was stormed by the 61st Regiment and Belooch Battalion, upon which occasion he, with a sergeant of the 61st Regiment, spiked one of the enemy's guns."

He rose to the rank of surgeon in November, 1857, and surgeon-major 1871. He served with his regiment during the troubles in the Bengal, Madras and Bombay presidencies, and also in Mauritius, Singapore (Straits Settlements), and the West Indies.

In 1879, Surgeon-Major Reade became a brigade-surgeon, and in the following year a deputy surgeon-general. In 1882 he was appointed P.M.O. of the Eastern District, and in 1886 Surgeon-General of the Southern District.

Decorations.

1. Indian medal and clasp for Delhi.
2. The Victoria Cross.
3. Companion of the Bath.

V.C. CAMPBELL MELLIS DOUGLAS, M.D.

BRIGADE-SURGEON.

CAMPBELL MELLIS DOUGLAS is the son of the late George Mellis Douglas, M.D., formerly Medical Superintendent of Quarantine, at Grosse Isle below Quebec, where he was born. His education was begun at Quebec and completed at Edinburgh. In 1862 he entered H. M. 24th Regiment of Foot as assistant-surgeon, and was gazetted, in due course, in 1863. Two years later he went to Burmah with his regiment. As medical officer, in charge of a detachment of troops, he was despatched to the Andaman Islands, a convict-station, where Lord Mayo was assassinated, It was while he was at this place that he won the Victoria Cross.

It was awarded to Campbell Mellis Douglas, M.D., Private Murphy, Private Cooper, Private Bell, and Private Griffiths, " for the very gallant and daring manner in which, on the 7th May, 1867, they risked their lives in manning a boat and proceeding through a dangerous surf to the rescue of some of their comrades who formed part of an expedition which had been sent to the Island of the Little Andaman, by order of the chief commissioner of British Burmah, with the view of ascertaining the fate of the commander and seven of the crew of the ship *Assam Valley,* who had landed there, and were supposed to have been murdered by the natives.

"The officer who commanded the troops on the occasion reports, 'about an hour later in the day Dr. Douglas, 2nd battalion, 24th Regiment, and the four privates referred to, gallantly manning the second gig made their way through the surf almost to the shore, but finding their boat was half filled with water they retired. A second attempt made by Dr. Douglas and party proved successful, five of us being safely passed through the surf to the boats outside. A third and last trip got the whole of the party left on shore safe to the boats.'

"It is stated that Dr. Douglas accomplished these trips through the surf to the shore by no ordinary exertion. He stood in the bow of the boat and worked her in an intrepid and seamanlike manner, cool to a degree, as if what he was then doing was an ordinary act of every-day life. The four privates behaved in an equally cool and collected manner, rowing through the roughest surf when the slightest hesitation or want of pluck on the part of any of them would have been attended with the gravest results. It is reported that seventeen officers and men were thus saved from what must otherwise have been a fearful risk if not certainty of death."

In 1872, Dr. Douglas became surgeon, in 1874 surgeon-major, and brigade-surgeon in 1882.

In all he served seven years in India. He married a Miss Burmester of Halifax, niece of Vice-Admiral Sir Edward Belcher.

Decorations.

1. The Victoria Cross.
2. The Silver Medal of the Humane Society.
3. The Cross of the Order of Knights Templar of St. John of Jerusalem.

COLONEL ARMINIE SIMCOE HENRY MOUNTAIN, C.B.,

ARMINIE SIMCOE HENRY MOUNTAIN was born at Quebec on the 4th of February, 1797. He was the son of the late Bishop Mountain, of Quebec. His military education was completed in Germany, according to the continental school. By dint of industry and a natural faculty he became an expert linguist, and thoroughly familiar with several oriental as well as European languages. This stood him in good stead in his future career.

On the 20th July, 1815, he had entered the service as ensign, rising to a lieutenancy three years later.

His first responsible position was as military secretary to Sir C. Halkett, in India.

In 1826, he had become major, and finally, in 1840, lieutenant-colonel.

Throughout the war in China he served as deputy adjutant-general to Lord Gough, and he was present at the first capture of Chusan, at the storming of the heights and forts upon Canton, at the action of the 30th of May, the taking of Amoy, the second capture of Chusan, and at the storming of the fortified heights of Chinae.

He also took part in the taking and defence of Ningpo, and in the action at Teske. In the desperate capture of Chapoo he received three very severe wounds.

He was present at the assault and capture of Chin Kiang Foo, and at the landing in Nankin.

At the termination of the war he returned to England with H. M. 26th. This regiment had suffered so much that it had become somewhat disorganized. Recruiting it in England, he soon made it worthy of its reputation.

Subsequently he returned to India as A. D. C. to Earl Dalhousie, Governor-General, and in a short time he received the appointment of adjutant-general.

At Chilianwallah, Colonel Mountain had the command of a brigade, and the terms in which Lord Keith thanked him for the famous charge that won the victory, testified to the position he had gained as a soldier. At this time he received the honourable appointment of A. D. C. to Her Majesty the Queen.

He was then placed in command of a division under General Sir W. Gilbert, and was sent in pursuit of the enemy after the battle of Goojerat.

Whilst on the march with the Commander-in-Chief he died of jungle fever, in the month of January, 1854.

Concerning him, the Commander-in-Chief made the following remarks: "Doubtless the important duties of the department over which Colonel Mountain has presided through a course of five years have been filled with equal punctuality by various predecessors, and with equal regard for the discipline of the army; but rarely, if ever, exhibiting that intimate blending of urbanity of demeanour and considerate feeling, with unflinching steadiness of purpose and impartiality unswerving in the performance of those not infrequently onerous and painful duties.

"The Commander-in-Chief has no need to record for information in India, or of Her Majesty's Army generally, that the able official adviser and friend whose loss he is deploring, served as head of the same department throughout the Chinese war of 1840-42, and held command of the brigade throughout the Punjaub in 1848-49, was with the force under Sir Walter Gilbert in command of a division, and uniformly acquitted himself in each of these important trusts with sound judgment and soldier-like ardour, which never failed to animate him wherever the opportunity offered.

"In all the social relations of life Colonel Mountain made himself extensively beloved and universally respected and esteemed. And Sir William Gorman feels well assured that his departure will be sincerely and deeply regretted by members of all classes and orders of society, in India as well as at home."

COLONEL SIR ÉTIENNE PASCHAL TACHÉ.

This distinguished native of Quebec was one of the aides-de-camp to Her Majesty the Queen.

COLONEL CHARLES W. ROBINSON, C.B.,

IS a son of the late Sir John Beverley Robinson, Bart., Chief Justice of Upper Canada. He was born at Toronto on the 3rd of April, 1836. His earlier education was obtained at Upper Canada College and at Trinity University, from which he graduated. Entering the Imperial military service, as ensign, in the Rifle Brigade, in November, 1857, he remained in that corps till 1885. His first period of active service was in the Indian Mutiny, through which he served in the second battalion of the brigade. During the Ashantee War he served from December, 1873, as brigade-major to the European Brigade, being present at the battles of Amoaful and Ordahsu, and at the capture of Coomassie. For his services in this campaign he was mentioned in the despatches and raised to the rank of brevet-major. In the Zulu War of 1879, for his gallantry at the battle of Ulundi, he was again mentioned in the despatches and received a brevet lieutenant-colonelcy. In 1884 he became a full colonel and went on half-pay in the following year, succeeding to several staff appointments.

For a time he was Military Instructor at Sandhurst, then Deputy-Assistant Adjutant-General at Aldershot, and brigade-major there. At present he is Assistant Military Secretary at the Horse-Guards in London. Of this appointment the *London World* of April 2nd, 1890, says:

"It is not too much to say that no appointment made for years past to the headquarters of the staff has given more general satisfaction to the service than that of Colonel C. W. Robinson, as assistant military secretary. Few staff-officers who have served at Aldershot have left behind them a better record. Under his able direction the adjutant-general's office was a model of what such an office should be, and as the assistant military secretaryship should at all times be filled by a courteous soldier, there is a sense of satisfaction in feeling that if Major-General Moncrieff's loss is regretted, his place is being supplied by one who possesses all the qualities necessary to secure that confidence which has made the Horse-Guards for years past a most popular department of the Army."

He married the daughter of General Sir Archibald Alison.

Decorations.

1. Medal and clasp for Indian Mutiny.
2. Medal and clasp for Ashantee War.
3. Medal and clasp for Zulu War.
4. Companion of the Bath.

SURGEON-GENERAL J. B. C. READE, C.B.,

WAS born at Perth, Ontario. He is a son of the late Staff-surgeon G. H. Reade, of that place. He is at present Assistant Director-General, Army Medical Department, in London.

SIR CHARLES STUART, BART.,

WAS born in Quebec, and served for a time in the 1st Regiment of Foot. He is now living in England.

SIR ALLAN NAPIER MACNAB, BART.,

A.D.C. TO HER MAJESTY THE QUEEN.

ALLAN NAPIER MACNAB was born at Niagara, in Canada, in the year 1798. His father who had fought during the Revolutionary War in the United States, had married, on retiring, a lady of Quebec. Throughout the American War, Allan Napier MacNab assisted very materially in repulsing the enemy and driving them out of Canada.

He had entered the Navy on board the man-o'-war of which Sir James Yeo was captain, and had cruised in her for some time during this unsettled period. Promotion was too slow in the Navy, he thought, so he joined the 100th Regiment under Colonel Murray. In the advance-guard he took part in the storming and taking of Fort Niagara.

From the 100th he exchanged into the 49th. He was present, with his regiment, at the destruction of the city of Buffalo, and in the attack upon Plattsburg, in the state of New York. He commanded the advance-guard at the Sarnac Bridge. After this he became a colonel of militia.

Of the taking of the *Caroline* and her destruction, Alison in his "History of Europe" says:
" This bold act which reflected equal honour on the judgment and courage of Colonel MacNab was decisive of the present fate of British North America."
He was created a baronet in 1856.

LIEUTENANT-COLONEL EDMUND LEE STREET,

BORN at St. Andrews, N. B., son of James Street, Esqr. This officer is now a lieutenant-colonel in the 11th Regiment of Foot.

LIEUTENANT-COLONEL HEAD

WAS born in the Province of Nova Scotia. Entering the British service he went in the 93rd Regiment against New Orleans. In 1877 he became Assistant Quartermaster-General to the force before Kolapore in South Mahratta. He is the author of " The Overland Route to India."

K

COLONEL EDWARD KENT STRATHEARN BUTLER,

A godson of his H. R. H. the Duke of Kent, was a native of Nova Scotia. After serving in the Imperial Army abroad for many years, he returned to reside in his native province, where he died.

LIEUTENANT-COLONEL R. G. NEWBIGGIN

Was born in Toronto, and served with the 89th Regiment through the Indian Mutiny. He was present at the affair at Honoria, and was for a time staff-officer to a field-force in pursuit of Tantia Topee and the Rao Sahib in Rajpootana.

MAJOR DE SALABERRY, C.B.

CHARLES MICHEL DE SALABERRY was born at the Manor of Beaufort, in Quebec, in 1778, and was the eldest son of the Seigneur du Sault Montmorency.*

He entered the British Army at the early age of fourteen, and began service in the Indies. He served there eleven years and took part in the siege of Fort Matilda under General Prescott who gave him command of the evacuation of that place. Then, as officer in command of the Grenadiers, he was ordered to Martinique.

De Rottenburg having chosen him as one of his aides-de-camp, de Salaberry went with him into the campaign in Holland. Thence he entered the Peninsula under the Duke of Wellington. At the siege of Badajos he greatly distinguished himself, and also at Salamanca, in the 60th Light Infantry, of which he became major.

Some short time after this he was apprised of the danger in which his native country was from the

---

* *Histoire des grandes familles françaises.*

hostility of the Americans, between whom and Great Britain war had broken out.

Without delay, he returned to Canada, and succeeded in raising the celebrated regiment of *Voltigeurs Canadiens*, with whom he won the decisive battle of Chateauguay. From his intrepidity, he was named "the Canadian Leonidas."

For this engagement the Imperial Government struck a gold medal and conferred upon Major de Salaberry the Companionship of the Bath, which was transmitted with an autograph letter from H.R.H. the Prince Regent.

The history of the life of the Duke of Kent is intimately connected with the de Salaberry family, with different members of which a correspondence was kept up by H. R. Highness, throughout a period of twenty years. Three other sons of Seigneur de Salaberry died abroad in the British service.

GEORGE SHEAFFE MONTIZAMBERT,

SENIOR MAJOR OF H.M. 10TH REGIMENT OF FOOT.

ATTACK ON MOOLTAN.

" The following officers had fallen in the siege-operations during the attack on the out-post, unrivalled for desperate gallantry in the annals of the Army, namely : Colonel Pattoun, of the 32nd Regiment of Foot, and Major Montizambert, of the 10th do., in the action before Mooltan on the 12th of December."—*News from India in The Times.*

GEORGE SHEAFFE MONTIZAMBERT was born in the city of Quebec, in 1813, and was the third son of the Hon. Louis Montizambert, a prominent Canadian.

He entered the Army in 1831, as ensign, joining H.M. 41st Regiment, which was then at Moolmein in the Arracan country.

He was with his regiment till 1840, when he returned to England on furlough, for the purpose of his own further military education.

When the troubles of 1842 began in Affghanistan he was in Quebec. Without delay he applied for the vacant adjutancy of his own corps and received the appointment. He then rejoined the 41st at Kandahar.

At this time an unfortunate accident happened him in the breaking of his leg. However, being determined that this should not balk him, he gave orders that he should be carried in a litter with the army to Ghuznee.

Having recovered sufficiently to take his place as adjutant, he continued the march to Cabul and through the Khyber Pass to Peshawur, and across the Punjaub to Ferozepore.

He took part in the actions of Goaine and before Ghuznee, in the occupation and destruction of that fortress, and of Cabul. He was also in the expedition into Kohistan, and at the storming and capture and destruction of Istallif.

Of this expedition it has been said that "almost every day's advance was tracked in blood."

In 1842 he returned to England with his regiment. This inactivity was not to his liking, and he purchased his majority, joining the 10th Foot at Lahore and going with it to Mooltan. He took part in the attack, and, at the second assault, fell as a soldier should, in the thick of the fray.

Of him the surgeon of the regiment says: "On the night of the 10th inst., he led four companies of the 10th Regiment in a night attack against an outpost of the enemy, under a frightful fire, with such dauntless gallantry and coolness as to excite the admiration of all who shared the dangers with him, and, to the delight of all, returned uninjured. You are, I dare say, aware that the attack failed and was renewed again yesterday morning with successful results. My poor friend while bravely leading in front was shot through the lungs and never afterwards spoke. I was in the field and had him conveyed under cover with the least possible delay, but, alas! no art could save him. I did all in my power to revive him, if but for a few moments, without avail. He ceased to feel either pain or pleasure, and shortly after breathed his last, without suffering, I believe and with hope.

"I have sent him back to camp. His remains will be interred this evening by his brother officers and fellow soldiers, and if their deep and unaffected sorrow for his death, and sympathy for his widow, can soothe her mind when it becomes more calm, pray convey it to her. The very men who fell wounded near him and were waiting to have their wounds dressed, shed tears over their sunburnt cheeks, and refused all assistance until his fate was determined."

COMMANDER EDMUND B. VAN KOUGHNET, R.N.,

Is a native of Toronto, and is a son of the late Chancellor Van Koughnet. During the Zulu War he was in command of boats in a river-expedition, and was wounded in an attack on the enemy.

LIEUTENANT ALEXANDER JOHN LEITH, R.N.,

WAS born in Hamilton, Ontario. He served in the Navy for many years and is, at the present time, on the retired list.

MAJOR FREDERICK W. BENSON,

OF THE 17TH LANCERS.

THIS officer is a native of St. Catharines, Ontario, and is a son of the late Hon. Senator Benson. He served for many years in India, and has recently received the appointment of Garrison Instructor at Bombay.

MAJOR RICHARDSON

WAS born in Upper Canada. He entered the British service, in the 2nd Regiment, early in the present century. On the breaking up of the 2nd he was appointed senior-captain of the 6th Scotch Grenadiers. Anxious to take part in active service in Spain, he joined General de Lacy Evans's Brigade, the British Auxiliary Legion, having been most highly recommended by Sir Herbert Taylor. He then became major in the 4th Fusiliers of the British Legion.

He published the "Movements of the British Legion," which in some way excited the ire of General Evans. A life-long dispute ensued between them. The affair was discussed in the House of Commons in England. The whole question is reviewed in his "Personal Memoirs of Major Richardson."

He was a Knight of the Military Order of St. Ferdinand.

He returned to Canada and became an author of repute, dying some years ago.

MAJOR HENRY HILLYARD ANGUS CAMERON

WAS born in Toronto, 29th March, 1844, and is a son of the late Hon. John Hillyard Cameron. He went from Oxford into the Army. In the 16th or Bedfordshire Regiment, he served in Affghanistan, British India, Burmah, and Tongoo. As senior major of that corps he is now stationed at Hyderabad.

MAJOR GERRARD FORSYTH.

GERRARD FORSYTH was born in the city of Montreal. He served through the Crimean campaign, and was in the battles of Balaklava and Inkerman, and at the siege of Sebastopol and capture of the Quarries.

The regiment in which he was formed part of the storming column in the attack on the Redan, of the 18th of June. He was also in the attack at Kinbourn. He retired as major in 1856.

Decorations.

1. Crimean medal and clasps.
2. The Sardinian medal.
3. The Legion of Honour

MAJOR ANTOINE BABY.

WAS a son of the Hon. Jacques Duperron Baby. Having entered the 24th Regiment of Foot, he proceeded to India, where he rose to the rank of major of that corps. At this period he married, and, withdrawing from military life, settled in France, at Tours, where he died in 1863.

MAJOR LOUIS JOSEPH FLEURY D'ESCHAMBAULT.

WAS born in Montreal, in February, 1756. In his early years he became page to Louis XVI. At the the time of the French Revolution he was recalled to Canada. He then entered the British service, as ensign, in the 24th Regiment of Foot, under General Taylor. Exchanging into the 109th regiment he became major in that corps. General Carleton appointed him Superintendent of Indian Affairs in Canada where he died in 1824.

MAJOR FREDERICK GORDON MACKENZIE.

WAS born in the city of Montreal, and is a son of Gordon Gates Mackenzie, Esqr., and grandson of the late John Gordon Mackenzie, Esqr., of that city. He and his brother, Cortland Gordon Mackenzie, graduated at Woolwich. Shortly after entering the Army, in 1877, Frederick Mackenzie became lieutenant in the 2nd Dragoon Guards or Queen's Bays. He is now serving in India as major of a cavalry regiment.

MAJOR FREDERICK WELLS.

FREDERICK WELLS was born in the city of Toronto. His father was a member of the Legislative Council of Upper Canada.

He entered H.M. 1st Regiment of Foot in October, 1841, as ensign. In this corps he went through the Crimean War. As captain he took part in the battles of Alma, Balaklava and Inkerman, and in the siege of Sebastopol. For these services he received a medal and clasps, and from the Emperor of the French, the Grand Cross of the Legion of Honour. The 1st Foot is the oldest regiment in the British Army, having served under Gustavus Adolphus and Marlborough. It has a whole history of brilliant deeds attaching to it. It formed part of the division under General Sir Richard England at Alma and Inkerman.

At the close of the war Major Wells revisited his native city. On the 31st of October, 1856,* a large number of citizens assembled at the Town Hall to present Major Wells with an address and a sword.

The Semi-Weekly Leader.

His Worship the Mayor, John Beverly Robinson, read the following address:—

"The Corporation of the City of Toronto, representing the wishes and feelings of their fellow-citizens, have, by their unanimous vote, requested me to tender you their congratulations upon your safe return to your native city after undergoing the dangers and privations of the Crimean Campaign. It is with equal pride and pleasure that we welcome home a citizen of Toronto whose breast displays those honourable distinctions conferred not only by his Most Gracious Sovereign, but by Her August Ally the Emperor of the French.

* * * * * *

"The municipal corporation of your native city desires to mark their sense of your gallant services, and to convey to you some proof of their estimation more substantial than words. It becomes my pleasing duty in the name of the people of Toronto to present you with this sword. (Great applause.) Should the storm of war again rise, we feel assured that it will be drawn with distinction to yourself and with honour to your country."

Major Wells replied in a cordial and soldierly manner.

MAJOR PATTINSON.

RICHARD PATTINSON was the son of R. P. Pattinson, Esquire, of the town of Sandwich, in Upper Canada, where he was born. His service extended over a considerable period. He served for fifteen years in India, becoming Adjutant-General of the Cavalry at Alliwale. He took part in the battle of Mahrajepore, and served throughout the Sutlej Campaign. At the battle of Buddenwahl his horse was shot under him.

Shortly before the Crimean campaign he had come back to Canada, but he rejoined his regiment on the outbreak of that war, through the whole of which he passed.

He was made Governor of Heligoland in 1857.

His decorations consist of three medals for India, and the Crimean medal.

SURGEON-MAJOR KEEFER.

WAS born in Galt, Ontario. He served throughout the Affghan War of 1848-49.

CAPTAIN J. A. POPE.

WAS born at Niagara, in the Province of Ontario, November 30th, 1831.

At the early age of fifteen he became secretary to Dr. Gillkrest, the chief medical officer at Gibraltar.

From this place he went to the Island of Jamaica, where he was of service during the cholera epidemic of 1849-50, for which he was mentioned in the following despatch:

"KINGSTON, Jamaica, Dec. 9th, 1850.

"SIR,—In submitting the enclosed letter from Dr. McLean, the principal medical officer on this station, I do most earnestly solicit your attention to the statement therein contained, relative to Mr. Pope, a gentleman whose valuable services in a position you would hardly suppose could be made valuable (in the way they have been), were brought under my notice during the last two years in a most favourable point of view.

"But his merits have been more eminently conspicuous during the many and great difficulties experienced (and which have been detailed by another hand), by the visitation of the most awful malady, the cholera, in the island, and which I am bound to declare entitled him to all the support in my power to afford.

"I do most sincerely hope you will be pleased to give your patient attention to this representation, as nothing but a sense of the eminent and most extraordinary services performed by this talented individual could possibly induce me to address you in a strain of praise, unusual, perhaps, in military connections.

"It has seldom fallen to my lot to have an opportunity of witnessing more talent, zeal and ability displayed by any one person, and I beg to add, I know none more likely to make to his country a grateful return for any patronage or favour you in your good judgment might think meet to bestow upon one so highly worthy of it. I have etc., etc.,

"T. BUNBURY,
"Major-General.
"Right Honourable Secretary for War."

In recognition of this strong commendation a special grant was made him which, the regulations say, was without precedent.

During the Crimean war he became paymaster of the 47th Regiment. For his useful services in this position he received the Crimean medal, with clasps for the various battles of that campaign.

L

At Inkerman he had a very narrow escape from death. In the early morning he had risen and just gone out of his tent when a shell entering shivered his resting-place. Before Sebastopol, the 47th was in the thickest of the fight. At the time of the attack on the Mamelon by the French, this regiment was in the sanguinary and successful engagement of the Quarries.

After the war was over, Captain Pope exchanged into the 67th, and with it went all through the Indian Mutiny.

He then went to China, serving in the war with that nation until ill-health compelled him to return to England, where he died soon after.

Few men of his years saw more varied service than Captain Pope.

CAPTAIN PARKER,

BORN in Halifax, N.S., served throughout the battles of the Crimean war, and was killed in the breach at Sebastopol.

CAPTAIN DE MONTENACH

WAS born in Montreal. He rose to the rank of major in the British service, in India, and died in the year 1885.

CAPTAIN LOUIS GUY,

Son of the Hon. Louis Guy, Legislative Councillor and King's Notary, was born in Montreal. At a very early age he was taken over to France where he was admitted into the *gardes nobles* of Charles X., King of France. He then went to England, obtaining a commission in the 81st Regiment of Foot. Subsequently he was placed in command at Trinidad, where he died of yellow fever. His brother officers erected a monument at his grave.

CAPTAIN DRURY, R.N.,

COMMANDING H. M. S. BELLEROPHON.

THIS officer was born at St. John, in the Province of New Brunswick, and is the son of Charles Drury, Esquire, one of the old band of United Empire Loyalists.

COMMANDER CHARTERIS SIMONS, R.N.,

Was also born in the city of St. John, N. B., and is the son of the late Charles Simons, Esquire, of that place. He is a commander in the Navy.

CAPTAIN LOUIS BABY

Was one of the three sons of the Hon. J. Duperron Baby, who had entered the service. Entering the 24th Regiment, he became captain and went out to India. In some way he became involved in "an affair of honour," and was killed in the duel that succeeded. He was a man possessed of all the qualities of a brave and successful soldier.

CAPTAIN JOSEPH BOUCHETTE.

Joseph Bouchette was born at Quebec, in May, 1774. His father had educated him for the Marine, but not wishing to follow that branch of the service, he devoted himself to the Army. After some experience in command of the Royal Canadian Volunteers, he exchanged into the 7th Fusiliers. He rose rapidly in this regiment, of which he soon became adjutant, but withdrew to assume a position of importance in his native country.

CAPTAIN BULGER

WAS a native of Newfoundland. He entered the Army in the Royal Newfoundland Regiment of Foot, as ensign, in 1804; rising to the rank of captain, in 1815. His service was chiefly in the United States. He went through the war of 1812, and was present at the battles of Chrysler's Farm and at the relief of Michilimackinac. For his share in the capture, by boarding, of the *Tigris* and *Scorpion*, he received the naval war-medal and clasps. He died at Montreal, in 1858.

CAPTAIN JENKINS

WAS born in New Brunswick. He exhibited great gallantry at the taking of Ogdensburg in the American war, where he lost both arms. He was in command of the Glengarry Regiment.

CAPTAIN ALAN CAMERON.

BORN in Toronto, 12th October, 1850, is a son of the late Hon. John Hillyard Cameron. He became captain in the 71st Highland Light Infantry, but exchanged into the 91st Highland Regiment. He served in Scotland, Malta, St. Helena, and Cape Town, where he now is.

CAPTAIN ROBERTSON.

Is a son of the late Dr. Robertson of Montreal. He joined the 12th Regiment of Foot, in 1851, going into the Kaffir war, where he served with considerable distinction. Having exchanged into the 95th, he was at the siege of Sebastopol. When the mutiny broke out he went to India, taking part in many of the battles of that period.

Decorations.

1. Kaffir War medal.
2. Crimean War medal and clasp.
3. Medjidie, fifth class.
4. Medal for service in India.

COMMANDER WYATT RAWSON, R.N.

WYATT RAWSON was born in Quebec, where his father and one of his brothers are clergymen of the Church of England. This young officer, who was destined to render a peculiar service to the British arms in Egypt, entered the Navy, becoming naval-cadet, in April, 1867. In January, 1873, he had risen to a sub-lieutenantcy on board the *Active*, corvette, under Captain Sir William Hewett.

During the Ashantee War he was especially mentioned in the despatches for his energy and skill when serving with the Land Transport Corps. At the battle of Amoaful, in 1874, he was very severely wounded. For his services in this campaign he was raised to the rank of lieutenant.

He went on the British expedition of 1875-6, to the Arctic regions. His scientific researches on this occasion were recognized by his being made a Fellow of the Royal Geographical Society.

In January, 1877, he became lieutenant on board the *Alexandria*, flag-ship of Admiral Hornby. In October of the same year he was appointed to the royal yacht,

Victoria and Albert, and his name, at the time of his death, was on the books of that vessel. During the Egyptian campaign, he was naval aide-de-camp to Sir Garnet Wolseley, and his skill, in leading the whole column of Alison's Brigade to the Egyptian lines of Tel el Kebir, has been very favourably commented upon.

Sir Archibald Alison's Highland Brigade was made up of the 42nd, the 74th, the 75th, and the 79th Regiments. The march across the desert to Tel el Kebir began about half-past four in the afternoon. The following is a description of it by a sergeant of the 79th Regiment:

. . . "About 1.30 a.m.,* the march was resumed. The 79th was appointed the directing regiment, and Lieutenant Rawson. R.N., had the duty of guiding it by the stars. Clouds obscured the sky occasionally, but the North Star and part of the Little Bear remained visible. Another non-commissioned officer and myself had the honour of being told off to march on the flank, and we were, consequently, close to the directing guide, Lieutenant Rawson. We were ordered to take off our helmets and keep our eyes fixed on a certain star, and if it should disappear to inform him in a whisper. In less than an hour several dis-

---

* *Nineteenth Century Magazine*, March, 1890.

appeared, and, as they did so, Lieutenant Rawson indicated others for us to watch. The strictest discipline was now maintained, and silence rigorously enforced; save that occasionally a horse would neigh and another answer, not a sound was to be heard but the slow trampling of many feet on the sand, resembling the fluttering of a flock of birds. Once, a man on whom the rum had taken effect or whom the weird silence had made ungovernably nervous, suddenly broke out into wild yells. Sir Garnet immediately rode up and ordered the offender to be bayoneted, but the regimental surgeon interposed and begged leave to chloroform him instead. This was granted—the man was drugged into insensibility and left lying on the sand. After marching at a funeral's pace for about two hours, a twenty minutes' halt was commanded. As the orders were slowly passed from company to company, in a low tone of voice, they did not reach the flanks of the brigade, which continued in motion, retaining the touch till the extremities all but met in front of the centre, so that the brigade in effect formed a great hollow circle. This line had to be labouriously straightened out and re-formed in the pitchy darkness, and in all but silence, and it was a fine proof of discipline that this was accomplished in twenty-five minutes. The advance was resumed at

4.30. The slowness of the pace was very tiring, and, but for the necessity of the steady watching of the stars, I certainly should have been nodding in sleep as I moved, as many men were doing. Sir Archibald Alison, commanding the brigade, was close to Lieutenant Rawson, and, as the night waned and nothing was discerned, he was clearly beginning to fear that something was wrong. 'Are you sure, Rawson,' he asked in a low tone, ' that we are on the right track?' 'Yes, sir!' said Rawson, 'we have the North Star on our right, and———another whose name I did not catch, in our front, and soon we ought to be there or thereabouts.' Dawn was just breaking. I could dimly see some objects in the front of us, looking like a lot of Kangaroos, hopping backwards and forwards—they were Egyptian cavalry we afterwards learned. I nudged my companion, and Rawson whispered 'we are not far off now.' Suddenly a shout was heard, then two shots were fired from opposite our left front and a man of F company fell dead. No notice was taken of this, and the brigade marched on silently; every man was on the alert. All at once a whole sheet of musketry flashed out, lighting up the scene far to right and left. Above the crackle of the rifle-fire sounded loud the roar of artillery. Regardless of these portents, our regiments marched silently and steadily on. The order to fix bayonets was given; when it had been obeyed and the men sloped arms, the rattle of the bullets on the bayonets was like to the sound of hailstones striking against glass. . . . . " The 79th had marched quite one hundred yards with their rifles at the slope when the command, ' prepare to charge !' was given. Down came the rifles of the front rank of the unbroken line. The 'charge' sounded, and as the last note of the bugle died away, a tremendous cheer was raised, the pipes struck up the slogan, and with our gallant colonel in front, shouting ' Come on, the Camerons,' the ranks broke into double time, and still cheering, with all their power swept forward on the enemy's position. One of the pipers, just as he began to play, had his bag-pipes pierced by a bullet, and most discordant sounds escaped from the wounded instrument. 'Gude faith,' cried the piper, philosophically, 'but the bullet's a deevilitch sicht better through her wame than through mine.' "

It will be remembered how gallantly the field was won. Rawson was mortally wounded amongst the very first of those who sprang over the trenches and tried to climb the earthworks. As the poor fellow lay near the trench the general rode up to him, having heard of his wound, and in response to his kind words of consolation, Rawson said faintly, 'I led them straight, sir, didn't I?' In the *Gazette*, two days before his death, his promotion as commander appeared, for his "valuable and gallant services rendered at the battle of Tel el Kebir on the 13th instant, on recommendation of the general officer commanding Her Majesty's Forces in Egypt."

He died on board the hospital-ship *Carthage*, shortly after the battle.

CAPTAIN DOUGLAS, R.N.,

WAS born at Quebec, and was the son of Dr. Douglas of Grosse Isle. He entered the Navy in 1854 on board the *Boscawen*. His first important service was on the western coast of Africa, where he took part in an expedition against some native chiefs. In 1870 he went to Japan as Director of the Naval College then established there. He remained in this position for five years, when he became Commander of the *Serapis*.

In 1887 he took up his residence in London as member of the Ordnance Committee.

He was also commander of the *Egeria*. As captain of the *Edinburgh*, of the Mediterranean squadron, he is now serving on that station.

CAPTAIN LOUIS HORNE BAZALGETTE

WAS a native of Halifax, N.S., and was one of the seven sons of Colonel Bazalgette, who entered the British service. He entered the 24th Regiment of Foot, as ensign in 1838, served in the Punjaub Campaign of 1848-9, and was present at the passage of the Chunab and the battles of Sadoolapore and Chillianwallah, where he was severely wounded. He received the Punjaub medal with clasps.

CAPTAIN EVELYN BAZALGETTE

ENTERED the 95th Regiment, in 1853, as ensign. He served in the Crimean War, and was wounded at the battle of the Alma, for which he obtained the Crimean medal with clasps.

CAPTAIN WILLIAM JOSEPH BAZALGETTE

ENTERED the 37th Regiment of Foot in 1852, and became captain in 1854.

LIEUTENANT GEORGE BAZALGETTE,

OF THE ROYAL MARINES,

ENTERED the service in the Marines, becoming first lieutenant in 1854.

CAPTAIN DUNCAN BAZALGETTE

ENTERED the service as ensign, in the 69th Regiment, in 1840. He became captain in 1850.

CAPTAIN JOHN HENRY GAMBLE

WAS born in Toronto. He is a son of Clarke Gamble, Esqr., Q.C. He had risen to the rank of captain in H.M. 47th Regiment of Foot, when he died at Lundi Kotal, in the Khyber Pass.

LIEUTENANT-COMMANDER CHARLES E. KINGSMILL, R.N.,

WAS born in the town of Guelph, in the province of Ontario, in the year 1855. He is the eldest son of His Honour, the County Judge of the County of Bruce. He entered the Navy in 1869, as one of the nominees of the Governor-General of Canada. Upon his examination, for promotion to a sub-lieutenancy, he won a "double first." His next step was into the Queen's Yacht, from which he was promoted to a full lieutenancy. He has served in various ships, and the certificates which his commanders have given him bear excellent testimony. At Zeila, where he was called upon for the exercise of coolness and judgment, he gained the commendation of his superior officers and was thanked by Major Hunter.

When Captain Nicholls of H.M.S. *Cormorant* died at sea, on a southern cruise, Kingsmill brought that vessel home, and, on the 5th February, 1890, was placed in command of the *Goldfinch*, in which he is now serving upon the Australian station.

Medals.

The Egyptian and Khedive medals.

LIEUTENANT JOLY DE LOTBINIÈRE.

THIS brave and handsome soldier was one of the sons of Seigneur Joly de Lotbinière, of Quebec. His father held sway over one of those few remaining seigniories which were established before the cession of Canada by Old France, and which preserve, to a remarkable degree, the characteristics of the French before the Revolution.

Lieutenant Joly entered the British Service in the 32nd Regiment of Foot. Having gone to India with that regiment from Canada, he put in his period of service there and in due course got leave of absence. On arriving in England, he heard of the near approach of the outbreak of the Crimean war, and resolved at once to take advantage of this period of activity. Volunteering, he joined the 88th Connaught Rangers, and served in the Crimean War before Sebastopol. Whilst in the trenches he became disabled by sickness, and was sent back to England as an invalid.

When Lieutenant Joly had recovered sufficiently to travel, the war had ended. He then went to France, and was amongst those British officers who received such distinguished attention from the Emperor and Empress of the French.

As his furlough was expiring he made preparations for his return to his regiment in India.

He sailed in the *Lord Raglan*, and when out of port, just before landing, the first news of the appalling Indian mutiny reached him. In response to his most anxious inquiries as to the 32nd, he found that it was shut up in Lucknow. Preparations were being hastily made for its rescue.

The thought that his regiment was in the heat of conflict and in danger of annihilation, and that he, one of its officers, was away, preyed upon his mind to such an extent that he resolved to rejoin it at all hazards. The difficulty of such an undertaking as a journey from Bombay to Lucknow at this time it is unnecessary to describe. The country was overrun with rebels bent upon murder and destruction. Some account of his journey may be gathered from the following extracts from his journal, written in French, which was found, after the relief of Lucknow, lying on the ground. It was picked up and, being a large book with many blank pages, it was used by a bandmaster to keep his accounts in. Subsequently it was brought to England, and as a result of correspondence regarding Lieutenant Joly de Lotbinière, it has come into the hands of his brother, the Hon. H. G. Joly de Lotbinière, Ex-Premier of Quebec.

"CALCUTTA, 20th Aug., 1857.

"I have been here since the 15th, not without much hardship. Everything is topsy-turvy here. Out of 75 or 77 regiments of Sepoys three only have remained faithful. (Here follows an account of native atrocities of a peculiarly distressing and revolting kind.) I am in such a fever of military and warlike ardour as I have never experienced, and I burn to find myself amongst these wretches, sabre and revolver in hand. I swear not to show them any pity I am told to await the order to set out by water, but the order does not come. Sir Colin is our commander-in-chief. I am going to see him to-day in order that I may be sent by land. Notwithstanding the risk, for the whole country is in arms, General Havelock with a small force is making heroic attempts to deliver my regiment at Lucknow, whither I am hastening to depart.

"I believe the most glorious day of my existence would be that in which I should throw myself amongst the first into Lucknow, to meet my brave 32nd or perish, but it is thought they are all exterminated, as since the beginning of June they have received no tidings from them. . . . 10th Sept., 10 miles from Futtypore camp—

"A good number of events since the 20th August. I waited impatiently from the 25th for them to send me by steamer to Cawnpore, but finding I should have to wait some time, determined to get there by land, cost what it might. I informed the authorities, who refused me permission, assuring me that the road was impracticable, in the hands of the rebels, and that I should be massacred. I went for the brigade-major, one of my friends, and told him what I wished to do. He told me it was impossible, but seeing my determination told me that once I was on the road he would make it up with the general. I had received, the night before, a note from Lord Elgin's secretary desiring me to go and see him, which I did, and was very well received. He asked me a good deal about London news, and my family. I told him what I was going to do. He also assured me it was impracticable, and I replied that I was determined to do it. He promised to get some words written in my favour to General Outram, whose army I wanted to join, and which was marching on Cawnpore to join Havelock, thence on to Lucknow to release my poor regiment.

"I received to-night an invitation from Lord Carrington, the Governor-General, which I was compelled to refuse.

"Next morning, the 26th of August, I set forward, going by rail to Ramefuya, a distance of about 150 miles, thence I must journey in a post carriage —but such a difference from the horsed vehicles of Europe; we went sometimes only two miles an hour.

"Whilst preparing to set out I was surrounded by officers who assured me for the hundreth time that the road was impracticable, and that before I got twenty miles I should meet with the rebels, and if not killed be compelled to return, and so forth.

"I felt my resolve growing weaker whilst hearing from all sides so unanimous an opinion, but did not wish to abandon my grand idea, namely, to enter Lucknow with the army which was to free my regiment.

"I started at seven o'clock on a very dark night, the two or three first hours that passed being occupied by reflections sufficiently melancholy, and at last I made up my mind to die, my consolation being that they would at least see I did not fail for want of courage to join my regiment.

"Each man on the road was to me an insurgent, and I held my sword in one hand and my pistol in the other. I was so tired, for I had not slept the preceding night, that I gradually fell asleep and continued so for several hours, despite my anxiety. I have not time to enter into any long details respecting this adventurous journey. (Here follows a vivid description of the country through which he passed at night, and an account of the frequent alarms which kept him in feverish excitement, nor was he without narrow escapes from falling into the hands of the enemy.)

"I arrived at last at four o'clock in the morning at the sacred Ganges. I was horribly tired. (He arrives at Allahabad.) I went direct to the general's quarters. . . . He was rather abrupt and in bad humour. He told me he would employ me at Cawnpore. He had refused to read my letter from General Markham, saying he had no time.

"I spent the night in marching about, sadly reflecting on the little encouragement and recompense in the Army. I consoled myself by determining to make up for it at Lucknow. . . . This evening I again marched alone, followed by my horse, a little in advance of the band of the 90th. The music exercised a soothing effect upon me. . . when I heard myself addressed by an officer telling me that Colonel Napier, chief of the staff-major, desired to see me. I caused the order to be twice repeated, and then said to him, when I at last comprehended this incredible news :

"'You must be mistaken; the night is so dark, you take me for another. I am Lieut. Joly, of the 32nd.'

"'Yes, it is you he wants,' said he.

"Since there was no more room for doubt, I directed myself to the place indicated, saying to myself, 'Is it possible that they are at last thinking of me?' I came up to the general and saluted him, when he told me to place myself under the order of Capt. Orr, who was in the rear with the baggage. I saluted him and turned my bridle to the rear, but swearing that if they were going to place me as a sentinel over the baggage I should rebel.

"What! whilst the army was occupying and delivering the 32nd, I, an officer of that regiment, to be placed in the rear-guard over the baggage! Oh, no, you deceive yourself if you think you are going to do that.

"Fortunately I was soon undeceived, for they informed me that eight miles further on we were going with ten Sikhs and four officers, mounted, to surprise the village and arrest the chief."

The village was surprised, and by the consummate daring of this handful of men, the chief was taken. They then re-joined the main body. It was several days before the general and his officers could bring themselves to believe that Lieut. Joly was really with them in the flesh, so certain were they, when they considered the difficulties they themselves had encountered, that one man could never have succeeded in reaching them. At last, however, they saw that it was so, and everything was done to make up for the coolness of his reception.

On the 23rd of September, the British Relieving Force came within a short distance of Alumbagh (the-garden-of-the-beauty-of-the-world). The enemy were drawn up before the buildings in good position. They were eventually forced within the walls by Havelock, whilst Outram pursued those whom he had cut off from the main body. Many were killed, for the enemy were well armed and handled their guns with precision. It was resolved to take the place by assault, and it was at this time that Lieutenant Joly received his death-wound while fighting in the breach.

Of him, one of the defenders of Lucknow says: *
"He had joined Havelock's force, delighted at the prospect of again seeing his brother officers and his old regiment, and in having shared in the honour of their relief. But he was destined to enjoy the looked-for pleasure a few hours only. Dangerously wounded at the storming of Alumbagh, he expired in sight of his old friends in a short time after his arrival in the Re-

---

* Ruutz Rees.

sidency, more deeply regretted than if his death had occurred under ordinary circumstances."

The following is an extract from the diary of the late Dr. Macmaster of the 78th Regiment.

"October 6, Tuesday [279—86], 1857.

"Lieutenant Joly of the 32nd was shot, having received a ball intended for me, but which I escaped by getting behind a pillar, having seen the point of the matchlock thrust from between two shutters."

LIEUTENANT CHARLES McKAY.

CHARLES McKAY was born in the city of Montreal, in April, 1836. He was a son of the Hon. Thos. McKay, of Ottawa. Proceeding to Montreal he completed his preparatory education there, going to Edinburgh to finish. In May, 1855, he was gazetted to the 97th Regiment, now part of the Queen's Own. As lieutenant in this corps, he sailed for the Crimea, but the regiment did not arrive in time to take part. However, the Indian Mutiny broke out at this time and furnished him with an opportunity of engaging in active service. He journeyed to Benares where his regiment was in General Frank's division, moving to join Sir Colin Campbell in the march to Lucknow. The following extract from his journal will be interesting as an illustration of the character of the work:

" At about two p. m. on the afternoon of the above day (10th March), the 42nd and 93rd Highlanders stormed and took the Martinière. As soon as the Sepoys saw our Highlanders advancing across the open plain towards them, they made for the town in great style. While in the act of bolting, we favoured them with an unlimited amount of shot and shell, which, falling amongst a crowd of them, would knock scores of the brutes over. On the 11th, three companies, mine amongst the number, were marched towards the Ghoorkas on the left, and here we had no end of skirmishing for two days; we drove the fellows into the town, the bullets dropping thick amongst us, but fortunately wounding very few. On the evening of the 13th, we moved over to the Secundrabagh, and the 97th killed upwards of eighteen hundred Sepoys in this building; the place is full of human bodies, and here we had to sleep for the night. At eleven next morning, received orders to advance on the Kysabagh, which was choke-full of Sepoys; we trotted along at a pretty good rate and when going up the different streets they peppered us in great style. On each side of the road as we advanced nothing but dead 'niggers' were to be seen, for the live ones kept pretty well under cover and potted at us through loopholes, every house in the place being thoroughly loopholed. On our arrival inside the palace then commenced the game, for we had to fight the brutes through each room as we went along. In the act of doing so our Colonel Ingram, was shot through the head. Just fancy, fighting through rooms far superior to any in England, and the tables therein covered with gold and silver ornaments. Had hard fighting all that night and next morning—found my Colt's revolver useful—tumbled over two swell-looking Sepoys with it—kept on fighting till the 16th, when they all made their exit. I never slept out of my clothes from the 10th to the 20th, and for six nights at a time had not so much as one wink of sleep: we certainly had hard work for the number of days we were at it."

This gallant young soldier fell a victim to small-pox at Banda, at the age of twenty-three. His fellow-officers spoke of him with sincere regard and admiration.

At the end of a twelvemonth after his death, the following letter was received by his mother:

{ " No, 16587
" 12.   " (Lr. 115.)

" War Office, LONDON,
" August, 1860.

" MADAM.—I am directed by the Secretary of State for War to transmit to you herewith, a medal which has been granted for Lieutenant C. McKay's services as an officer of the 97th Regiment of Foot, to be retained in commemoration of his gallant conduct in the campaign in India. You are requested to acknowledge the receipt of the medal upon the form herewith enclosed.

"I am, Madam, your obedt. servant,
"B. Hawes.
"Mrs. A. McKay,
"Rideau Hall, Ottawa, Canada, America."

LIEUTENANT WM. DUNBAR SELBY,

A son of Wm. Dunbar Selby, M.D., was born in Montreal. He served in the 24th Regiment in India for some years. His health broke down and he retired, dying in Canada, in 1884.

MAJOR POMERET,

BORN at Montreal, served for many years in the 24th Regiment of Foot, and died abroad.

LIEUTENANT HENRY BEAUFORT VIDAL

WAS born at Chatham, Ontario, and entered the British Army as ensign in 1862. In 1864 he became lieutenant in the 4th Regiment and served in that regiment in the Mediterranean, India and in Abyssinia, where he was at the capture of Magdala. He is now major in "C" Company, Royal School of Infantry, at Toronto.

JOHN SEWELL

WAS born in Quebec of an old United Empire Loyalist family. He entered the Royal Navy at the age of thirteen. On his return to India he was gazetted to an ensigncy in H. M. 89th Regiment. From this he was transferred to H. M. 49th, serving in Canada. He served all through the war of 1812-13, and for his services was made adjutant of his regiment which was recalled to Europe on the opening of the second Napoleonic war.

He was considered one of the best swordsmen in the service.

During the Kaffir War he was commended for his valour. This was his last service. He was buried at Quebec in 1875.

LIEUTENANT STEPHEN W. SEWELL,

SON of the late Colonel John Sewell, late Captain of H. M. 49th Regiment, and grandson of the late Chief Justice Sewell, of Quebec. Entered the Imperial service in 1855, in the 86th Regiment of the line. His services were chiefly in India, and the following extract from a letter will give an idea of his most serious engagements:

"PALACE HOSPITAL, JHANSI,
April 27th.

". . . I suppose you will have heard by this time of my having been wounded on the 3rd inst. at the storming of this place. . . , I will now give you fuller particulars of the fight. . . . On the evening of the 2nd, there was a report in camp that we were going to attack the town of Jhansi at twelve o'clock that night. . . . The Brigadier came up and told us off into two parties, with the 25th N. I. as support. We were now marched rapidly in the direction of the town, when Coleman, adjutant, rode up to me and told me to ride like fun to the advance-post and bring in fifty of the Grenadier company. I turned my horse's head and went off like a shot. I never enjoyed a gallop so much. . . . The enemy opened a very heavy fire when we got to the wall and were putting up our ladders. The enemy kept throwing down huge stones upon us, besides firing briskly. . . . I got my ladder up in good time, but the brutes knocked it down again and at the same time smashed nearly all the rungs out of it with a huge rock. . . .

" We soon drove the enemy from the wall, and they retreated to the fort, fighting every inch of the ground. When we got to the fort we were exposed to a tremendous fire from both flanks and front. An officer who had been in the Crimea said he never saw a heavier fire, even before Sebastopol. The niggers came out in thousands, . . . and we drove them back at the point of the bayonet. Here I was wounded and carried back to camp. (Here follows an account of several attacks.)

". . . Now we expect six companies of the 71st here to-morrow. Simpson and Bonham and a lot of fellows in Quebec are with them. . . . We took several elephants here; one was an enormous brute said to be a hundred and fifty years old. He had bars of pure gold on his tusks, valued at £500. He was in a great state of excitement when I first saw him, owing, I suppose, to the noise. He was breaking great branches off the trees about him and throwing them at our men. . . .

" (Sgd.)   S. W. Sewell."

For this he was named for promotion by the Commander-in-Chief in his despatches. He died the 2nd of April, 1861, from injuries received while steeple-chasing at Anullabad in India, through the falling of his horse.

HONOURABLE HENRY AYLMER

Is the second son of Lord Aylmer, of Melbourne, in the province of Quebec, where he was born. He entered the Royal Marine Artillery, as cadet, in 1859, and retired as lieutenant in 1870. Since then, as colonel, he has devoted himself to the interests of the Canadian militia.

MATTHEW AYLMER,

SON of Lord Aylmer, born in March, 1842, entered the 7th Royal Fusileers as ensign, in 1861, retiring as lieutenant in 1871. He is now a major in the Canadian militia,

CAPTAIN JONES HASPER READE,

BORN in Perth, Ontario, was a son of the late G. H. Reade, lieutenant-colonel of the Canadian militia, and a brother of V.C. Surgeon-General H. T. Reade He served throughout the Crimean campaign in the 3rd Buffs, in which he held a captain's commission.

LIEUTENANT WILLIAM CHARLES READE,

BORN at Perth, Ontario, was a son of the late G. H. Reade, lieutenant-colonel of the militia of Canada. He joined the 1st West India Regiment, and died in the tropics.

LIEUTENANT FREDERICK SHORTLAND, R.N.,

WAS born at St. Andrew's, in the province of New Brunswick. This officer was on board the *Huascar* in her encounter during the late Chilian War. He was also at the storming of Alexandria, and has the Egyptian War medal and Khedive's star.

VERNON JONES, R.N.,

WAS born at St. Andrew's, N.B. He was an officer on board the war-vessel chosen to take the Duke of Edinburgh in his first trip round the world. He took part also in the surveys of the north-eastern Atlantic coast, in H.M.S. *Columbia*.

LIEUTENANT JOHN DENISON, R. N.,

WAS born in the city of Toronto, and is the son of the late Lieutenant-Colonel G. T. Denison, of the militia. He is lieutenant in command of H.M.S. *Firebrand*.

PAYMASTER REGINALD C. HODDER, R.N.,

Is a native of the city of Toronto, and son of the late Dr. Hodder. He is paymaster on H.M.S. *Comus*.

LIEUTENANT W. A. R. DE CHAIR, R.N.,

A NATIVE of Montreal, is serving on board H. M. S. *Inflexible*.

LIEUTENANT ARTHUR ROMEYN BECK, R.N.,

WAS born at Peterborough, Ontario, and was the son of the Rev. J. W. R. Beck, M.A. He entered the Navy in the *Royal Alfred*, flagship, at Halifax, in 1869. He served in the *Britannia*, the *Bellerophon* and the *Ariadne* on the Mediterranean station. He was gazetted lieutenant in February, 1881, and was despatched to the West Indies station in the *Atalanta*. In this vessel he sailed in June, 1881, for Portsmouth, and since that date nothing has been heard of his ship. It is thought that she went down with all hands in mid-ocean.

LIEUTENANT HALE,

SON of the Hon. Jeffrey Hale, of Quebec, served in the British Army in foreign lands.

LIEUTENANT L'ECYER,

IN the 60th Regiment of Foot.

CAPTAIN IRVING GRANT,

Of Quebec, father of Baron de Longueil in the British peerage, served in the British Army.

CHARLES JOHN MOOR DE BIENVILLE,

Of Quebec, served in the 3rd King's Own Light Infantry.

CAPTAIN DE LANAUDIÈRE,

Of Quebec, served in the Canadian Contingent of Burgoyne's army in the American War.

LIEUTENANT DAN. D'HERTEL,

Of Quebec, served in the Canadian Contingent of Burgoyne's army.

LIEUTENANT SIDNEY AUGUSTUS BAZALGETTE, R. A.

This officer served in the Artillery in the Crimean War; was at the siege of Sebastopol, and in the expedition against Kinbourn. He received the Crimean medal and clasp.

JAMES ARNOLD BAZALGETTE

Served in the 42nd Royal Highlanders at Sebastopol. He became paymaster of this corps in 1855, and received the Crimean medal and clasp.

JAMES DE LILLE, M.D.,

Son of the High Constable of Montreal, served, unattached, throughout the Crimean war.

LIEUTENANT GUY.

Lieutenant Guy was born in Montreal, and was the son of the Honourable Louis Guy. He entered the

81st Regiment of Foot, as ensign. For a time, he occupied the position of Deputy-Adjutant-General of Quebec. Subsequently he returned to his regiment in Bermuda, where he died of yellow-fever, in 1841.

LIEUTENANT BREHAUT

WAS born at Quebec. The service of this officer is of very old date, and all that is, at present, known of him is that he served under the British flag and died abroad.

CAPTAIN CAMPBELL,

BORN at the Manor House of St. Hilaire, in Quebec. He served in the 74th Highlanders for a time and then became Secretary to Lord Campbell, in Canada.

FRANCOIS VASSAL DE MONTIRET

WAS born in Quebec. He served throughout the war in Holland under the Duke of York, and also under Burgoyne, in America. He returned to Canada and succeeded the Honourable François Baby, as Adjutant-General of Lower Canada.

LIEUTENANT HIGHWOOD JOHNS,

BORN in Canada, served as lieutenant in the 18th Royal Irish Regiment through the Maori war of 1864. He was accidentally killed at Malta, where, in an attempt to make a leap from one wall to another, he fell.

LIEUTENANT PYKE.

WAS born at Halifax, N.S. This officer served in the army under the Duke of Wellington in Spain, where he was killed.

LIEUTENANT FAWSON.

WAS born at Halifax, N.S. This officer was killed at Spain, whilst serving in the British army, during the Peninsular War.

LIEUTENANT GREEN, R.N.,

WAS born in Nova Scotia, and was a grandson of the Honourable Benjamin Green, who administered the government of that province, in 1766. He was present at the battle of Trafalgar, and for his services received a medal. His scientific attainments were of a high order.

LA CORNE SAINT-LUC

WAS born in Lower Canada, and came of a fighting family. He was a master-spirit of the Indians, and led those who fought under Burgoyne against the Americans. Saint-Luc was once taken prisoner by the enemy but released.

In a letter of 1777, General Tryon writing to Lord George Germaine, speaks of Saint-Luc as a fit leader of the savage allies that he proposed to hurl upon the Americans. Saint-Luc had vowed vengeance for his captivity, and General Tryon said, " *Pour soi-même, il m'a assuré qu'il ne voudroit jamais, jamais (jusqu' à ce que son ame Bat. dans son Corps et le Sang coule dans ses Veines) oublier les Injures et les Insults qu'il a reçue de ces gueux.*"* He has been roundly abused and

---

* Haddon's Journal.

he has stoutly defended himself. He died in October, 1874, in his native province.

JAMES SHAND DUNCAN, M.D.,

WAS born in the city of Montreal, and was a son of the late James Duncan, Esqr., the well-known artist of that city. He entered the 81st Regiment, and became surgeon of it. He served for a lengthened period during the insurrections in India.

GEORGE DUNCAN, M.D.,

WAS a brother of James S. Duncan, M.D. He became assistant-surgeon of the 81st Regiment, serving in India.

SAMUEL HOLLAND

WAS born in the province of Quebec. He joined the 60th Regiment of Foot, as ensign. He was killed in a duel, near Montreal, in 1799, by a bullet from one of the pistols which General Wolfe had given his father.

THEODORE JUCHEREAU DUCHESNAY

Was born in Quebec, on the 2nd of April, 1846. He is a son of the late Narcisse Juchereau Duchesnay, Seigneur of Beauport, in Quebec.

In 1858 he was gazetted lieutenant in the 100th Prince of Wales's Royal Canadian Regiment, subsequently exchanging, in 1860, into the 75th King's Own Borderers. Whilst in that regiment he served for three years at Gibraltar, as well as in other places. He was afterwards appointed by the Imperial Government to a military position in Canada, which he still holds.

DOCTOR BUCKLEY,

A native of Quebec, served throughout the Crimean War as surgeon.

LIEUTENANT W. G. VAN INGEN, R. N.,

WAS born in Toronto. This officer is at present on the *Orontes*, trooper.

COMMANDER DANIEL McNAB RIDDELL

Is a son of John Riddell, Esquire, of Hamilton, Ontario, in which city he was born. At present he is in the *Pelican*, on the North American station.

ROYAL MILITARY COLLEGE, KINGSTON.

THE following list contains names of those, of Canadian birth, who have gone through the Royal Military College, Kingston, Canada, and are now serving. Some of the first batch of graduates from this college did not turn out at all creditably, for reasons of a personal and painful nature, and left the service. Fortunately, this condition of things did not continue, and the college now stands well in the estimation of the War Office.

CAPTAIN H. M. CAMPBELL, of Frederickton, N. B., of the Royal Artillery, stationed at "Drake's Island," Plymouth.

CAPTAIN H. B. MACKAY, of Kingston, Ont., of the Royal Engineers.

CAPTAIN J. W. SEARS, of St. John, N. B., of the South Staffordshire Regiment, at the "Curragh," Ireland.

CAPTAIN E. J. TAYLOR, of Montreal, of the Cheshire Regiment, in Burmah.

LIEUT. H. E. WISE, of Kingston, of the Cameronians, Scottish Rifles, at Lucknow, Bengal.

LIEUT. W. J. MCELHINNEY, of Brockville, Ont., of the Royal Highlanders, Bombay.

LIEUT. G. M. DUFF, of Kingston, Ont., of the Royal Engineers, in Bengal.
LIEUT. W. G. STAIRS, of Halifax, N. S., of the Royal Engineers, at Aldershot. This officer was lately with Mr. H. M. Stanley in Africa, in his transcontinental journey.
LIEUT. G. M. DUFFUS, of Halifax, of the Royal Engineers, at Kurrachee, India.
LIEUT. F. ST. D. SKINNER, of Hamilton, Ont., of the Royal Sussex Regiment, at Ferozepore, in Bengal.
LIEUT. W. H. ROBINSON, of St. John, N. B., in War Office, London.
LIEUT. A. JOLY DE LOTBINIÈRE, of Quebec, of the Royal Engineers, in Bengal.
LIEUT. H. C. NANTON, of Cobourg, Ont., of the Royal Engineers, in Bengal.
LIEUT. J. J. LANG, of St. Mary's, Ont., of the Royal Engineers, at Halifax, N. S.
LIEUT. P. G. TWINING, of Halifax, N. S., of the Royal Engineers, in Bengal
LIEUT. J. A. MOREN, of Halifax, N. S., of the Royal Artillery, at the Royal Military College, Kingston Ontario.
LIEUT. C. F. ALMON, of Halifax, N. S., of the Royal Artillery, Quettah, Bengal.
LIEUT. C. R. HODGINS, of Toronto, Ont., ot the Royal Artillery, in Bara Gully.

Lieut. J. H. Laurie, of Halifax, N. S,, of the King's Own Royal Lancaster Regiment, at the Infantry School, Toronto, Ontario.

Lieut. H. Sloggett, of Charlottetown, Prince Edward Island, of the Royal Engineers, at Plymouth.

Lieut. J. N. C. Kennedy, of Peterborough, Ont., of the Royal Engineers, at Jamacia.

Lieut. G. M. Kirkpatrick, of Kingston, Ont., of the Royal Engineers, at Chatham.

Lieut. G. S. Cartwright, of Pinegrove, Ont., of the Royal Engineers, at Aden.

Lieut. H. C. Smith, of Quebec, of the Royal Dublin Fusiliers, at the Quebec Infantry School.

Lieut. G. S. Worsley, of Quebec, of the Bengal Staff Corps, in Bengal.

Lieut. C. P. Hensley, of Charlottetown, P. E. I., of the Royal Dublin Fusiliers, at Fusseerabad, Bombay.

Lieut. E. R. C. Girouard, of Montreal, of the Royal Engineers, at Woolwich.

Lieut. C. M. Maxwell, of Quebec, of the Royal Artillery, at Newport.

Lieut, P. H. Casgrain, of Quebec, of the Royal Engineers, in Bengal,

Lieut. E. O. Smith, of Montreal, of the Northamptonshire Regiment, in the Straits Settlements.

ROYAL MILITARY COLLEGE, KINGSTON.

LIEUT. K. B. CAMERON, of Toronto, Ont., of the Princess Louise Argyle and Sutherland Hussars, at Aldershot.

LIEUT. A. P. BREMNER, of Halifax, N. S., of the Royal Engineers, at Halifax, N. S.

LIEUT. W. J. TILLEY, of Belleville, Ont., of the Royal Engineers, in Bengal.

LIEUT. E. J. DUFFUS, of Halifax, N. S., of the Royal Engineers, at Cawnpore, India.

LIEUT. T. C. SKINNER, of Woodstock, Ont., of the Royal Engineers, at Malta.

LIEUT. R. J. MACDONALD, of Victoria, British Columbia, of the Royal Artillery, at Woolwich.

LIEUT. A. ADAMS, of Ottawa, Ont., of the Royal Engineers, at Chatham.

LIEUT. G. B. LAURIE, of Halifax, N. S., of the Royal Irish Rifles, in Egypt.

LIEUT. E. C. VAN STRAUBENZEE, of Montreal, of the Royal Artillery, at Gibraltar.

LIEUT. E. V. O. HEWETT, of Halifax, N. S., of the Queen's Own (Royal West Kent Regiment), at Malta.

LIEUT. C. S. COWIE, ot Halifax, N. S., of the Royal Scots (Lothian Regiment).

LIEUT. W. C. G. HENEKER, of Sherbrooke, Quebec, of the Connaught Rangers, at Dinapore, Bengal.

Lieut. H. C. Carey, of Victoria, British Columbia, of the Royal Engineers, at Halifax, N. S,

2nd Lieut. H. G. Joly de Lotbinière, of Quebec, of the Royal Engineers, at Gibraltar.

2nd Lieut. E. C. Hamilton, of Montreal, of the 3rd King's Own Hussars, at Ballincollig.

2nd Lieut. W. B. Lesslie, of Kingston, Ont., of the Royal Engineers, at Chatham.

2nd Lieut. C. B. Farwell, of Sherbrooke, Quebec, of the Royal Engineers, at Chatham.

2nd Lieut. G. M. Johnston, of Quebec, of the Royal Artillery, at Halifax, N. S.

2nd Lieut. J. E. L. Baker, of St. John, N. B., of the Royal Artillery, in Egypt.

2nd Lieut. A. E. Panet, of Ottawa, Ont., of the Royal Engineers, at Chatham.

2nd Lieut. A. M. Cayley, of Whitby, Ont., of the Royal Artillery, at Gibraltar,

2nd Lieut. A. G. Bremner, of Halifax, N. S., of the Royal Engineers, at Chatham.

2nd Lieut. C. G. Murray, of Halifax, N. S., of the Connaught Rangers, at Malta.

2nd Lieut. H. S. Rogers, of Peterborough, Ont., a descendant of that Imperial officer, Major Rogers, of "Rogers's Rangers," who, as commander of the "British Expedition," took over the French forts in America, at the close of the French war.

2ND LIEUT. H. B. D. CAMPBELL, of Quebec, of the Royal Engineers, at Chatham.
2ND LIEUT. R. C. MORRIS, of Perth, Ont., of the Royal Artillery.
2ND. LIEUT. C. M. DOBELL, of Quebec, of the Royal Welsh Fusiliers, at Lucknow, Bengal.

THE CANADIAN VOYAGEURS.

THESE men were chiefly volunteers who came forward when the call was made by England for boatmen for the Nile expedition, in the late Soudan war.

In regard to Canadian volunteers, General Wolseley, who served in Canada as commander of a Red River Expedition, wrote to Dr. Schultz, of Winnipeg, as follows:

"GOVERNMENT HOUSE,
"CAPE COAST CASTLE,
"12th November, 1873.

"DEAR DR. SCHULTZ.—Your letter of the 5th September last has just reached me. . . . I wish I had a thousand Canadian volunteers here at this moment, for with such a force I think I should be able to bring the King of Ashantee to terms. At
o

present I am too weak to undertake offensive operations, and must wait till I obtain soldiers from England. . . .

"Believe me to be very faithfully yours,
"(Sgd.) G. F. WOLSELEY,
"Dr. Schultz, M.P., Winnipeg."

LIEUTENANT-COLONEL FREDERICK C. DENISON,

OF the Canadian militia, a son of the late Lieutenant-Colonel G. T. Denison, of the militia, and a native of Toronto, was appointed by the Imperial Government to the command of the contingent of Canadian boatmen in the late Soudan War. At the close of the campaign General Brackenbury thanked Colonel Denison and the Canadians for the part they had taken in this arduous expedition. He is a brother of Lieut.-Col. G. T. Denison of the militia, of Toronto, who wrote a well-known work upon cavalry,

P. O. JOSEPH HEBERT,

A NATIVE of Quebec, entered the Egyptian Campaign 1882, attached to " N" Battery, 2nd Brigade. He died of fever at Cairo.

COMMANDER LINDSAY, R.N.

CHARLES GOWAN LINDSAY, son of William Burns Lindsay, Clerk of the House of Commons of Canada, was born in the year 1840, at Quebec. He entered the Navy in H.M.S. *Camperdown*, at the age of fourteen. His first important command was in the *Harpy*, tender to Admiral Boxer's flag-ship, at the time of the Russian war, in the Baltic Sea. His lieutenant was the now distinguished officer, Admiral Commérell. Then he became Lieutenant of the *Hannibal*. He was at the siege of Sebastopol and the storming of Kinburn. In 1861 he was made Commander of the *Galatea*. In due course he succeeded to the command of several vessels, and was sent upon many important missions. He died at St. Servan, France, in 1871.

Medals.
1. The Crimean Medal.
2. The Turkish Medal.
3. The Baltic Medal.

MAJOR WILSON,

AT present commanding "B" Battery, Quebec, is the eldest son of the late William Wilson, Esqr., of Kingston, Ontario. At the outbreak of the Soudan war he was desirous of going to Egypt, and, as an officer of the Canadian militia, he applied to the war office. He was attached to the 1st Battery 1st Brigade, Southern Division, R.A. On the march to the relief of General Gordon, when General Stuart's column had reached the Nile it was reinforced by two steamers that General Gordon had sent down from Khartoum. These steamers bore six brass cannon and two hundred and fifty Soudanese gunners.

The command of this contingent was given to Major Wilson. When Khartoum had fallen and the campaign had practically ended, Major Wilson was given command of troops, invalids, and despatches for England. On his arrival he had the honour of being presented to Her Majesty the Queen.

For his services in the Soudan he received the Queen's Medal with clasp, and the Khedive's Star.

List of Authorities.

Army, New List, *Hart.*
Army List, *Hart.*
Arrow, the Broad.
Admirals, Lives of, *Southey.*
Admirals, Three British, *Rev. Dr. Brighton.*
Army, The British, *Archer.*
Army, The British, *Scott.*
Affghanistan, Sale's Brigade In.
Affghanistan, Dennie's Campaign in.
Army, Regiments of the British, *W. Richards.*
Admirals, Lives of, *Dr. J. Campbell.*
Affghanistan, War in, *Kaye.*

Biographia Nautica, *John Kent.*
Biographical, Royal Nav., *Supp.*
Beckwith, Life and Labors Amongst the Waldenses of Piedmont, *Rev. J. Meille.*
Beckwith, Despatches.
Beckwith, Wesleyan Magazine.
Burgoyne, Fonblanque's Political and Military Episodes of.

Cross, The Victoria, *O'Byrne.*
Cross, The Victoria, *Toomey.*
Chronicle, The London.
Courier, The Boston.
Chronicle, The Quebec.
Canadians, Celebrated, and Persons Connected with Canada to 1862, *H. J. Morgan.*
Canada, History of, *Bell.*
Case of the Colonists, *Godlonton.*
Canada, History of, *Smith.*
Canadian News, The.

Canada, Eight Years of, *Major Richardson.*
Canada Le.
Cyclopædia of Canadian Biography.

Delhi (Letters), *Turnbull.*

Europe, History of, *Alison.*

Gazette, Naval and Military.
Gazette, Army and Navy.
Gazette, The London.
Gazetteer, Naval, *Marshall.*
Gazetteer, Naval, *Nore.*
Guards in Canada, The, *Major Richardson.*

Historical Records of the British Army, *Cannon.*
History, Naval, *James.*
History of Reign of George III., *Adolphus.*
Haddon's Journal and Orderly Books.
Histoire des Grandes Familles Françaises.

Illustrated London News.
Illustrated News of the World.

Journal of Lieut. Edmond Joly de Lotbinière.

Kaffir and Kaffir Wars, *Lieut.-Col. Napier.*
Kars, Siege of, *H. Sandwith, M.D.*
Kent, Duke of, Life of, *Dr. Anderson.*

LIST OF AUTHORITIES.

Kent, Duke of, Correspondence with de Salaberry.

Letters, to the author from Lady Darling, Lady Willshire, Admiral Sir Provo Wallis, G.C.B.; Col. Montizambert, J. LeMoine, Esqr., F.R.S.C.; Christopher Robinson, Esqr., Q. C.; Mrs. Robinson-Owen, Sir Adams Archibald, Hon. H. G. Joly de Lotbinière, Major Crawford Lindsay, Hon. Mr. Justice Baby, J. Akins, Esqr., S. F. Huestis, Esqr., Rev. Wm. Brighton, Major Wilson, War Office, Admiralty Office, S. Farmer, Historiographer; Major-Gen. Cameron, C.M.G.; Major Mayne, R. E.; 🜨.☾. Surgeon-Gen. Reade, Miss Boulton, Major Vidal.

Lucknow, Siege of, *R.P.Anderson.*
Lucknow, Defence of, *by a Staff-Officer.*
Lucknow, Siege of, *Ruutz Rees.*

Miscellany, *Bentley's.*
Military Scrap-Book.
Memoirs of Basil Hall.
Mémoires sur le Canada.

Memoirs of Major Richardson.
Mountain, Life of, *by his wife.*

Nova Scotia and Nova Scotians, lecture before Literary and Debating Society, by Rev. Mr. Hill, A.M., 1858.

Navy List, Royal.

Punjaub Campaign, *Archer.*
Peninsular War, History of, *Napier.*
Pamphlet, Canadian.

Review, Edinburgh.
Records, Admiralty.
Records, War Office.
Records, Public.

Soudan, War in the, *Haultain.*

Tientsin Massacre, *Thin.*
Times, The
Travels of Duc de la Rochefoucauld in North America.

United States, History of, *Bancroft.*

Wellington, Life of, *Maxwell.*
War of 1812, *Major Richardson.*

INDEX.

	PAGE		PAGE
Aylmer, H., Hon	216	DeSalaberry, Major	171
Almon, C. F.	229	DeBienville, Chas	220
Adams, A.	231	DeLanaudière, Capt.	220
Aylmer, Matthew	216	D'Hertel, Lt.	220
		DeLille, Surg.	221
Beckwith, Chas., General	104	De Montiret, F.	222
Belcher, Ed., Sir	124	Duncan, J. S., Surg.	225
Baby, General	138	Duncan, Geo., Surg.	225
Bazalgette, Lt.	221	Duchesnay, Col.	226
Bazalgette, A., Lt.	221	Duff, G. M., Lt.	229
Brehaut, Lt.	222	Duffus, G. M., Lt.	229
Buckley, Surg.	226	Duffus, E. J., Lt.	231
Bouchette, Jos., Capt.	188	Dobell, C. M., 2nd Lt	233
Bulger, Capt.	189	Denison, F. C., Lt.-Col.	234
Bazalgette, Louis, Capt.	197	D'Eschambault, Major	179
Bazalgette, Evelyn, Capt.	197	De Montenach, Capt.	187
Bazalgette, William, Capt.	197	Drury, Capt.	187
Bazalgette, D., Capt.	198	Douglas, Capt	196
Bazalgette, G., Lt.	198	Denison, Lt.	218
Beck, A., Lt	219	De Chair, Lt.	218
Baby, A., Major	179		
Baby, Louis, Capt.	188	England, General	131
Butler, Col.	170		
Benson, Major	176	Forsyth, Major	178
Bremner, A. P., Lt.	231	Farwell, C. B., 2nd Lt	232
Baker, J. E. L., 2nd Lt	232	Fawson, Lt.	223
Bremner, A. G., 2nd Lt	232		
		Guy, Capt.	187
Cameron, Major	178	Gamble, Capt.	198
Cameron, A., Capt.	190	Grant, Capt.	220
Campbell, Capt.	222	Guy, Lt.	221
Campbell, H. M., Capt.	228	Green, Lt.	224
Cartwright, G. S., Lt.	230	Girouard, E. R. C., Lt.	230
Casgrain, P. H., Lt.	230		
Cameron, K. B., Lt.	231	Head, Lt.-Col.	169
Cowie, C. S., Lt	231	Hale, Lt.	219
Carey, H. C., Lt.	232	Holland, S.	225
Cayley, A. M., 2nd Lt.	232	Hodgin, C. R., Lieut.	229
Campbell, H. B, D., 2nd Lt.	233	Hensley, C. P., Lt.	230
		Hewett, E. V. O., Lt.	231
Drummond, General	111	Heneker, W. C. G., Lt.	231
Dunn, W.C. Col.	141	Hamilton, E. C., 2nd Lt.	232
Douglas, W.C. Brig.-Surg.	158	Hebert, P. O.	235

INDEX.

	PAGE
Hodder, Reg	218
Inglis, I. E. W., Sir, General.	44
Jenkins, Capt	189
Joly de Lotbinière, Lt	200
Jones, Vernon	218
Johns, H., Lt	223
Joly de Lotbinière, A., Lt	229
Joly de Lotbinière, H. G.. 2nd Lieut	232
Johnston, G. M., 2nd Lt	232
Keefer, Surg.-Major	183
Kingsmill, Lt	199
Kirkpatrick, G. M., Lt	230
Kennedy, J. N. C., Lt	230
Leith, Lt	176
L'Ecyer, Lt	219
Lang, J. J., Lt	229
Laurie, G. B., Lt	231
Lesslie, W. B., 2nd Lt	232
Lindsay, Com	235
Mountain, Col	161
McNab, Allan, Sir	168
Montizambert, Major	173
Mackenzie, Major	180
McKay, Chas., Lt	209
Mackay, H. B., Capt	228
McElhinney, Lt	228
Moren, J. A., Lt	220
Maxwell, C. M., Lt	230
MacDonald, R. J., Lt	231
Morris, R. C., 2nd Lt	233
Murray, C. G., 2nd Lt	232
Newbiggin, Lt.-Col	170
Nanton, H. C., Lt	229
Owen, E. W. R. C., Admiral.	114
Pattinson, Major	183
Pope, Capt	184
Parker, Capt	186
Pomeret, Major	212
Pyke, Lieut	223
Panet, A. E., 2nd Lt	232

	PAGE
Regiment, 100th	9
Reade, Ð. Œ. Surg.-Gen	156
Reade, J. B. C., Surg.-Gen	167
Robinson, Col	165
Richardson, Major	177
Robertson, Capt	190
Rawson, Com	191
Riddell, Com	227
Robinson, W. H	229
Rogers, H. S., 2nd Lt	232
Reade, Capt	217
Reade, Lieut	217
Stuart, General	139
Stuart, Sir Chas	167
Street, Lt.-Col	169
Simons, Com	188
Sewell, John	213
Sewell, S. W., Lt	214
Selby, Lt	212
St. Luc Corne	224
Sears, J. W., Capt	228
Stairs, W. G., Lt	229
Skinner, F. St. D., Lt	229
Sloggett, H., Lt	230
Smith, H. O., Lt	230
Smith, E. O., Lt	230
Skinner, T. C., Lt	231
Shortland, Lt	217
Taché, Étienne, Sir	164
Twining. P. G., Lt	229
Tilley, W. T. Lt	231
Taylor, E. T., Capt	228
Van Straubenzee, Lt	231
Van Ingen, Lt	227
Van Koughnet, Com	176
Vidal, Major,	212
Voyageurs, Can	233
Williams, Fenwick, Sir, Gen..	22
Wallis, Provo, Admiral	72
Westphal, Admiral	95
Worsley, G. S., 2nd Lt	230
Wise, H. E., Lt	228
Wells, Major	181
Wilson, Major	236

www.ingramcontent.com/pod-product-compliance
Lightning Source LLC
Chambersburg PA
CBHW021404230426
43666CB00006B/631